RAYMOND TC

Life Shaping
Spirituality

*Treasures old and new for
reflection and growth*

www.kevinmayhew.com

First published in Great Britain in 2014 by Kevin Mayhew Ltd
Buxhall, Stowmarket, Suffolk IP14 3BW
Tel: +44 (0) 1449 737978 Fax: +44 (0) 1449 737834
E-mail: info@kevinmayhewltd.com

www.kevinmayhew.com

ISBN 978 1 84867 696 1
Catalogue No. 1501424

Cover design by Justin Minns
© Images used under licence from Shutterstock Inc.
Edited by Nicki Copeland
Typeset by Richard Weaver

Printed and bound in Great Britain

Contents

Dedication

For my darling grandson
Joseph Michael James Cullen
in celebration of his baptism.

Acknowledgements

I have the enormous privilege of ministering at Ripon College Cuddesdon, Oxford, and what I have learned from the community there has enabled this book. So many thanks to the ordinands and the staff for all the inspiration, help and encouragement I have had with this project.

Special thanks to the Revd Canon Professor Martyn Percy, College Principal, for his generous support of my learning, my ministry and my writing projects. Thanks to those whose stories and experiences of Christian spirituality traditions have contributed to the book, especially the Revd Sister Helen Julian CSF, the Revd Tom Carson, the Revd Andrew Lightbown and the Revd Jeremy Putman. Many thanks to David Cowie for patiently reading the manuscript to see if it made sense before I submitted it for publication.

Many thanks to all at Kevin Mayhew and especially to Nicki Copeland for her patient editing of my work. Last, but by no means least, many thanks to my dear wife Rose, in this the fortieth year of our marriage, and to all my family for their loving and generous support.

About the author

Raymond Tomkinson began working with ordinands at Ripon College Cuddesdon, Oxford, in 2005 as a Visiting Spiritual Director and has been College Chaplain since Trinity Term 2009. He spent some time in religious life before becoming a State Registered Nurse specialising in the care of elderly people and in hospice care. He was a hospital manager and staff development officer before training for ordained ministry. He has been a parish priest in the Church of England and director of a diocesan retreat centre. He is sought out for spiritual direction and to lead retreats.

In 2010 Raymond was awarded an MA in Ministry from Oxford Brookes University. His research topic explored how ordinands secure a curacy at the end of their training at Cuddesdon. He has made a particular study of spiritual direction and the potential of music as a vehicle of trans-cendence as evidenced in the compositions of Mozart (his favourite composer).

Raymond now lives in Rutland with his wife, Rose, near his daughter and her family. He teaches and writes on Christian spirituality and prayer. Works published by Kevin Mayhew include *Come to Me: A Resource for Weary Christians and Those Who Care About Them* (2000), *God's Good Fruit* (2002), *God's Advent People* (2003), *Clothed in Christ* (2008) and *Hard Time Praying?* (2009). He is a contributor to *Sermons on Difficult Subjects* (2011) and *Services for Special Occasions* (2012). His most recent book is *Called to Love: Discernment, Decision-Making and Ministry*, published by SCM Press in 2012.

Introduction

Background

For several years I have been teaching Christian Spirituality with women and men training for ordained ministry at Ripon College Cuddesdon, Oxford. I draw on the writings of contemporary as well as classic authors in the field, but the real challenge comes from the ordinands themselves, who come from a wide range of church traditions and with varying experiences of spirituality and prayer. I encourage them to explore their own identity in relation to God and the world about them, to appraise their knowledge and experience of different spirituality styles and traditions in the worldwide church (both historical and contemporary), and to reflect on where they may now be drawn personally as they journey further in Christian faith and discipleship. I aim to raise their awareness of Christian spirituality, to offer practical ways of living prayerfully, to encourage further study and experimentation, and to help prepare them for ministry to people seeking advice and guidance about their own spirituality and its expression. I offer a smorgasbord: tasters of a range of spirituality traditions in the hope that such savoury samples might whet the appetite for further exploration and learning.

In this book I offer a similar strategy: it is an overview of some spirituality traditions and some ideas for exploring and expressing spirituality in worship and prayer. I hope to provide a resource for those who seek a Christ-centred life and a deeper relationship with God.

It has been my privilege, through a ministry of spiritual direction, to have accompanied women and men from a wide range of Christian traditions as they have sought to make sense of their own identity, of life and of their relationship with God and the world around them. This experience of spiritual accompaniment has also informed this book. It is offered as a resource for others who accompany or support pilgrims in their Christian discipleship.

Challenge and change

So often, issues about a relationship with God are presented as problems. The story is told of being restless or bored with worship or dissatisfied with ways of praying. God may seem to have disappeared, or life events have crowded out consciousness of God. Perhaps, in spite of strenuous effort, God seems absent, or it may be difficult for us to look God in the eye: to notice that God is beckoning us in a different direction or bidding us face up to something. Sometimes, as the story unfolds and signs and symptoms are described, it becomes clear that the way someone related to God before a certain life event or in an earlier time of Christian discipleship no longer works for them. What was once 'salt' has lost its taste.[1]

People change: they grow, they mature. Life events shape their perspective on God and on life in general. Behaviour changes, political or social views change, values change; but people are not always aware that their spirituality, too, has changed. Much depends upon what they believe their spirituality to be. In this book I explore, with the reader, what spirituality might be. I point out that authorities in the field regard all definitions of spirituality as unsatisfactory and incomplete. Indeed, to define spirituality is to circumscribe

---

1. Mark 9:50.

it, to constrain it. I draw the reader towards both a position of contentment with non-definition as well as an acceptance that spirituality changes, even as everything else in life changes, and that the root of the problem may be that recent experience or understanding of our spirituality, its expression and articulation in prayer no longer resonate. It may be time to reassess who we have become, and to recognise how the landscape of our Christian discipleship has changed; there may be new and life-enhancing ways of relating to God, to people or to the world in general. Perhaps two-dimensional 'cartoons' of God that saw us safely through early spiritual or religious nurture no longer work for us. For that reason we may currently be experiencing difficulties. We may accuse ourselves of losing our faith, a state for which we may blame ourselves. We might imagine that a state of spiritual *ennui* is the consequence of a God who no longer cares about us or who does not understand our current life circumstances. It is time to move on, but to where might God be drawing us?

Deep calling on deep

Perhaps we sense a call to a deeper relationship with God, with others, with creation, and we need a little encouragement to respond to that call by being open to new or unfamiliar ways of relating to God. It may be that the spirituality or tradition which characterised our early nurture in prayer no longer serves us well and we are searching for an articulation of who we have become before God, or we may be seeking permission to abandon a prayer practice or habit that no longer seems effective. For example, a deep desire to move from vocal prayer to contemplative prayer is not uncommon, but early Christian nurture may have left us with unhelpful mores.

Treasures older and newer

Many Christians are unaware of much of our worldwide Christian heritage, especially if such treasures originate beyond their own denominational or church experience. Through reflection on some of the spiritual 'greats' in the Christian heritage I hope that the reader might be tempted to explore their lives, examples and teaching. The aim is to offer tasty samples of untried spiritual nourishment or to encourage the reader to rediscover long-forgotten spiritual food. I use story (both fictional and fictionalised factual accounts with permission) to illustrate situations and circumstances with which the reader might resonate.

Within the limitations of this book there is not scope to write in depth about even some of the major spirituality traditions, so I offer an overview of some of them, especially those which have left us a legacy of accessible and helpful practices. For example, when advising on how one might keep perspective during a challenging life event, the reader is encouraged to explore what the Ignatian discipline of *The Examen* might have to offer. When considering spirituality in the context of church community or family life, the reader is encouraged to explore what the Benedictine tradition might have to offer.

Is this book for me?

This book is for all Christians: those who believe themselves to be 'stuck' and those who don't know that there are spiritual riches to be discovered amongst treasures older and newer that have been cherished by fellow Christians around the world. Here is an opportunity to taste and see how good the Lord has been, and an encouragement to explore what 2000 years of Christian spirituality might have to offer. This is a book for all who seek a deeper relationship with God and an authentic spirituality in their Christian discipleship. It is a book for all who accompany others on their spiritual journey. It is a book for those undertaking study or research in the field and those who teach them. It is a book for those who are struggling to understand why they feel as they do, and who long for a sustained and meaningful relationship with God in the context of their own everyday life as the person they have become. It is a book for those who have undertaken a faith nurture course or programme who have more questions about God and prayer.

I make no distinction in the book between ordained and lay people unless it is strictly relevant to the point being illustrated. I am struck, however, by Gordon Jeff's chilling remark that,

> I think we also need to be realistic and to remind ourselves that apart from public worship many clergy have, themselves, effectively given up praying with dire, long-term, [consequences] results to their ministry.[2]

Helping clergy and those in training for ministry to sustain prayer is of great importance to me, but I don't want to limit the scope of the readership by exclusively addressing their needs, no matter how pressing. I hope, however, that clergy and ordinands will find the book helpful for themselves and for those to whom they minister.

---

2. G. Jeff (2007), *Spiritual Direction for Every Christian*, 2nd edition, London: SPCK, p.15.

CHAPTER ONE

Definition-defying spirituality

John had recently come to faith and, although he had found helpful the faith nurture course that had brought him to commitment to Christ, he found himself with questions about prayer and about relating to God and the world around him. His minister encouraged him to seek out a spiritual guide who could help him with his explorations. As he journeyed to meet her, he rehearsed in his mind how he would describe his way of praying and the difficulties he was experiencing. After a warm greeting, his guide listened to the story of his journey in faith. Then she said, 'So tell me, John, what gets you out of bed in the mornings?'

John was taken aback, and before he could think about his reply he blurted out, 'The smell of coffee and of frying bacon!' They shared their delight in the deliciousness of the little things in everyday life, and the time together passed quickly.

As he was leaving, John turned to his guide and said, 'I thought you would want to hear about my prayer time!'

His guide smiled encouragingly and replied, 'I will, John, but you know, God is interested in the whole of our life as we live it in him and for him and for those in whom we find him.' As he travelled home, John felt excited about the adventure before him: a journey deeper into the God who had become so important to him in recent times.

It is so tempting to think of spirituality as being only about prayer or pious practices when the reality is that our spirituality encompasses the whole of our life and finds expression in our prayer, in our relationship with God and in the people around us: indeed, in relation to the whole of creation! It is tempting to try to define spirituality, but we are likely to conclude that there is no fully satisfactory definition. The need to define it seems to stem from two motives. The first is that people like definitions: they offer boundaries and make vast topics manageable. It would seem that dictionaries are full of them! Or are they? Often a dictionary will simply offer words or phrases that are associated with the topic, or they offer metaphors or similes when attempting to describe the seemingly indescribable.

The second reason why writers and speakers on Christian spirituality suggest definitions is because they offer a perspective, a starting point for a journey into the unknown which may not lead to a place of definition but which will have offered an interesting landscape and made the journey worthwhile, even if the destination remains tantalisingly out of reach. If or when we do finally reach the journey's end, we find it is a place beyond definition but, having arrived there, we are encouraged to rest, to relax in that space and to overcome our human need to define, as we surrender our desire to know and to own the unknowable and the indefinable.

If those who guide us to this point achieve this, they will have brought us closer to the truth of the matter and, by so doing, they will have saved us from a depreciation of spirituality, a fragmentation of it. They will have helped us to avoid one of the pitfalls in a secular understanding of spirituality: that spirituality is a question of being about one thing but not about another; that it is about being something ethereal, out there, distinct from the reality that embraces the whole of human life in God. Separating things spiritual from things temporal is the beginning of not only a fruitless journey but also a descent into dualism and, ultimately, despair. Only by embracing spirituality as indefinable can we truly know what it is about.

In a parallel and not unconnected example, can we satisfactorily define God? Dictionary definitions simply offer us words like 'Other', 'deity' or 'overarching being', but that does not take us very far. Jesus and the apostles have revealed something about what God is like, and their descriptions are available to us in Holy Scripture. We are taught that God is love,[3] but can we satisfactorily define love? Paul teaches us how perfect love behaves,[4] but is that the same as knowing what or who the Christian God of love is, or how God is experienced? Paradoxically, we may not be able to define love, but we can reach out and touch it! We may not be able to define God, but we can know God's touch as it is experienced in our loving relationships.

Perhaps it may help to think of spirituality as being rather like holding a prism up to the light and asking a few people what colour it is. Depending on where they are standing and where the light is coming from, the prism will appear to be a particular colour. All would agree that the prism appears to be different to each person. Each can bear the truth of how others see it, and they will all agree that the prism is solid and real and of itself. They will also agree that the colour will change as the light changes and that there will be changes, too, if the prism changes shape, like when a diamond is cut and polished it changes shape and form. The beauty and the wonder of it will change according to its setting and the light shining upon it.

There is in us a healthy desire to understand and to apprehend, so it is not surprising that we might want to define

---

3. 1 John 4:16b.
4. 1 Corinthians 13.

spirituality. Are we not like children trying to cup fog in our hands so that we can wonder at it? Yet we get by without satisfactory definitions; indeed, we hold the very indefinability of God to be an attribute or characteristic of God! I am asking the reader to do the same in respect of spirituality: to hold that spirituality is indefinable as a means of steering us away from attempting to circumscribe it, to compartmentalise it or to contain it to the exclusion of anything else in relation to God, ourselves, other people or the whole of creation. Instead, I would encourage the reader to work with the dynamic of spirituality in its relation to God, in relation to the whole of human life to the exclusion of nothing and to hold that *Christian* spirituality is the regeneration of all life in Christ, vivified by the Spirit of God who is at work renewing and transfiguring all things in Christ: things 'seen and unseen'.[5]

I once asked 100 Christians – women and men aged between 23 and 61 – this question: 'What is spirituality?' No two people offered the same definition. Phrases such as 'the Spirit within me' and 'relating to God' linked spirituality with belonging and being in God. Phrases such as 'how I pray' and 'my response to God' gave spirituality functionality: something to do rather than something to be. Others responded with single words such as 'being', 'identity' or 'energy'. These give spirituality an ontological rather than a functional quality but do not link spirituality with God. When the 100 respondents were given an opportunity to compare responses, they quickly adopted the definitions of others as they resonated with their own reflections and welcomed other words or phrases with which to articulate something that defied full

---

5. Nicene Creed.

expression. The more they shared their reflections the more expansive became the definition, yet satisfaction with the outcome continued to elude them. In conclusion they were happy to live with the question not satisfactorily answered while recognising that others may ask them the same question, and they were glad of an opportunity to reflect on how they might respond to it.

To the question, 'What is *Christian* spirituality?' the answers of the 100 Christians were generally Christocentric: 'It is no longer I who live, but it is Christ who lives in me.'[6] There was general agreement that spirituality, for a Christian, is about human identity in relation to God, that it is a living and dynamic dimension of humanity infused with the Spirit of God and that it is unique in each of us even as our personhood is unique. If the reader is not satisfied with this broad brush definition of spirituality, then my point is well made!

If our spirituality is both alive and dynamic and is the essence of us, regenerated in God, it will be subject also to response and reaction to life events and circumstances. We are not only reactive to our environment or to what we have learned or in the way we have been conditioned; we affect our own life and the lives of others by the choices we make, the values we hold and the way we practise our faith. Our spirituality is shaped not only by life events and circumstances but also by our encounters with the living God and our enlightenment by the Holy Spirit. Indeed, we hope for some reshaping as we seek to become more Christlike, as we allow ourselves to be grown into the image and likeness of God.

---

6. Galatians 2:20.

Spirituality and the essence of 'me'

Without settling for any unsatisfactory definitions we recognise that, as human beings with imagination, senses, feelings, intuition and gut reactions, we may legitimately use our limited human vocabulary to articulate what our own spirituality means to us. In Chapter five we will consider in more detail the 'us' rather than the 'me' of Christian spirituality: our belonging in the company of others and our connectedness to the Church as the Body of Christ. In this chapter and the next, however, we will consider our spirituality as we stand alone, each of us a unique creation. If our spirituality is the essence of 'me', then our unique and whole identity is our 'fragrance' – the unique combination of essences that comprise 'me'. Further, the reader is asked to consider not only that each is of us a unique fragrance but also that our fragrance changes throughout our life. Perhaps we could say that it is a bit like fragrances we might purchase on the high street: in our youth we may have been happy that a particular fragrance pervaded us and said something about us, but in later life a different fragrance seems to match who we have become. A *parfumier* would tell us that a particular fragrance is likely to change on application to the skin of each different person and that it will also change on that same individual in different circumstances.

Spirituality – the whole confection: Graham's opinion

Graham is in his early sixties and has been a practising Christian all his adult life. He spoke to me of people who have no religious practice but whom he considers to have a spirituality. I asked him what he understood 'spirituality' to mean. He thought for a few moments before saying, 'Spirituality is like an ice-cream wafer. The wafer biscuits are like the body and the ice-cream between them is like the spirit. The wafer biscuits have no purpose other than to hold the ice-cream.' I asked Graham if the wafer biscuits add anything to the confection. Emphatically, he answered, 'No' and (reflecting on the relationship of the body to the spirit) he said he had always considered the body to have no value other than to 'hold' the spirit during its life on earth.

In Graham there seems to be a disconnectedness between the things of the spirit and the things of the body, and a sense in which God seems to care only for the former and not for the latter. In other conversations Graham has spoken of family, work, relationships and his concern for the environment, but he regards God and prayer as the only essentially spiritual dimensions of life. My instinct and my learning made me want to encourage him towards an appetite for the deliciousness of God's gift of all created life, life in all its fullness, which is the combination of 'ice-cream' and 'wafer biscuits' – the whole glorious and God-given confection that is life!

In a subsequent conversation I discovered that Graham's early learning was coloured by St Paul's teaching on 'body' and 'spirit'. It was then that Graham separated the things of the spirit from the things of the flesh, rendering almost everything, except prayer, to the latter. Rowan Williams cites 1 Thessalonians 5:23 in this regard and suggests that it is fairly clear from the rest of St Paul's work that 'spirit' is very far from being simply an area of human experience or a portion of the human constitution.[7] He goes on to say that the major epistles make it plain that 'living in or according to the "spirit" is a designation of the entire set of human

---

7. R. Williams cited in Waller & Ward (1999), *An Introduction to Christian Spirituality*, London: SPCK.

relations, to God and each other and our environment.'[8] He acknowledges, however, that when St Paul writes of 'spirit', it is seldom clear whether this means simply and directly the Spirit of God or whether it includes ourselves as 'spiritual'. Waller and Ward, in the preface to the same book, state that the purpose of the book (which brings together, from a cross-section of Christian denominations, reflections on spirituality from some of the greatest theologians of our day) is to examine the principles behind the translation of 'spirituality' as 'life in the spirit' and to see how they can offer a new way forward in the search for a true, personal and dynamic 'spirituality' for today.

Ross Thompson, writer in theology and spirituality, discusses in some depth the relationship between theology and spirituality.[9] He would seem to agree that there can only be an authentic Christian spirituality where there is a theology. Spirituality is rooted and grounded in God, and God is to be found revealed in humanity and experienced in human life. Spirituality and its expression is more than what Thompson calls our 'bodily practices': prayers, liturgical practices, acts of worship.[10] It is more than any other vocal call upon God. It is what Wakefield describes as 'the way in which prayer influences conduct, our behaviour and manner of life, our attitudes to other people . . . It shapes dogmas, inspires movements and builds institutions'.[11]

We hold in tension intimacy and distance with God (this side of heaven), which has been described as an 'aching'[12] or a

---

8. Ibid, p.2.
9. R. Thompson (with G. Williams) (2008), *Christian Spirituality*, London: SCM.
10. Ibid, p.150.
11. G. S. Wakefield (ed.) (1983), *A Dictionary of Christian Spirituality*, London: SCM, preface p.5.
12. R. Rolheiser (1998), *Seeking Spirituality: Guidelines for a Christian Spirituality for the Twenty-First Century*, London: Hodder & Stoughton, p.3.

'restlessness'. It was famously described by Saint Augustine in one of his prayers: 'You have made us for yourself, Lord, and our hearts are restless until they rest in you.'[13] The 'energy' of 'aching' or 'restlessness' is part and parcel of the dynamic of the God–humankind relationship and symptomatic of a healthy spirituality. The Canadian priest and spiritual writer, Ronald Rolheiser, describes spirituality as 'what we do with our unrest' and 'about what we do with the fire inside us; about how we channel our eros.'[14] He suggests there is 'a fundamental dis-ease, an unquenchable fire that renders us incapable, in this life, of ever coming to full peace'.

Rolheiser writes accessibly yet profoundly with a logical, almost clinical progression. He writes, helpfully, of what makes for full, rounded and authentic Christian spirituality. His book addresses some of the advanced themes and issues facing spiritual directors and draws heavily on psychological and counselling models, and is helpful in raising awareness of the potential problems we may encounter either in our own spiritual journey or in that of those whose journey we share.

Aching, tension and restlessness are common feelings in our developing love affair with God. They are experienced in a positive way – as a 'pull' towards love, beauty, creativity and a future beyond our limited present. Desire can show itself as aching pain or delicious hope. Rolheiser suggests that spirituality is what we do with that desire. He suggests that what we do with our longings, in terms of handling both the pain and the hope they bring us, *is* our spirituality. He goes on to say that an unspiritual person is someone without energy or someone who has lost their identity.[15]

---

13. E. M. Blaiklock (tr.) (1983), *The Confessions of St Augustine*, London: Hodder & Stoughton.
14. R. Rolheiser, *Seeking Spirituality*, p.3.
15. Ibid, p.12.

Being 'lost' in this way implies an awareness that we know we are not where we should be. There are those, however, who wander, who have a nomadic spirituality and who, in their restlessness, do not know that they are seeking the right place to be. But what is meant by 'place'?

Healthy spirituality and being in the right place

The first 'place' to seek to be is in Christ who is in God – to be at one with God, through Christ. For Williams, 'the place of Jesus is finally the place of the Logos before the mystery of the Father; a mystery never fully penetrated or sounded.'[16] He suggests that 'the body itself is a kind of reflection of the spirit on the one hand, and the spirit itself, because it is created, even though it is always falling short of the full reality of God.'[17] The life of the spirit is reflected in the face of the believer, and it is that reflection that sometimes attracts others to the believer; the unspoken comment might be that 'this person has something I do not have and I want it!' Perhaps we could liken it to the face of Moses when he returned from the mountain.[18] Christ is the 'place' where we hold in tension our dis-ease and distance from God along with a sense of intimacy with God, who is so far above us that we cannot know him yet so deep inside us that we cannot escape him. It is also the 'place' from which to view the world around us, to try to view the world as God views it. We see the needs of God's people and hear their cry. We are inspired to help bring in God's kingdom of peace and justice where hunger and poverty will no longer exist, a subject to which we shall return in Chapter six.

---

16. R. Williams, cited in Waller & Ward, *An Introduction to Christian Spirituality*, p.5.
17. Ibid, p.6.
18. Exodus 34:29, 30.

The theologian Philip Sheldrake brings a philosophical dimension to the discussion when distinguishing between 'place' and 'a neutral space'. In his aptly subtitled book *Christian Living and the Doctrine of God*, Sheldrake attempts to reconcile what he understands to be a prolonged separation of spirituality and theology and the nature of the sacred. Framing his understanding in Trinitarian theology, he considers how the dynamic of God's action in the world relates to humankind's response. He describes the difference as being to do with 'meaning'. He writes:

> from a Christian perspective, 'meaning' implies that the world has theological significance and therefore implications for spirituality – the way people seek to live their beliefs . . . to say that the world has 'meaning' makes it a 'place' rather than a neutral space.[19]

It could be argued, therefore, that a person who, from the place they are in, sees the view purely in terms of 'neutral space' and not as having some meaning or theological significance and requiring some meaningful response from them, is spiritually anaesthetised. Sheldrake gives the example of the World War II concentration camp of Birkenau-Auschwitz, which 'brings into sharp, and for Christians, painful focus the intimate connection between the meaning of "place" and the quality of human relationships associated with it.'

Each of us must find our place in God and in the world. Both God and the world will shape who we are and how we behave. To be in the 'right place' is to be at one with God and our neighbour and to be able to hold, in tension or in balance, the relationship between the two and to live within

---

19. P. Sheldrake (1998), *Spirituality and Theology: Christian Living and the Doctrine of God*, London: DLT, p.165f.

the dynamic of God, knowing what it means to belong in God and to be a human being growing into God. This brings to mind the epigram of St Athanasius: 'Therefore He was not man, and then became God, but He was God, and then became man, and that to deify us', which is often translated as, 'God became man that man might become God.'[20] (Though some hold that St Irenaeus of Lyons said it first!)

Rolheiser[21] recognises the integrative quality of lived spirituality and cites evidence of the pattern of Jesus' ministry and teaching before giving examples of the consequences for spiritual dis-ease where there is an imbalance. He cites Jesus' teaching regarding 'three clear components to discipleship': prayer, fasting and alms-giving and goes on to explain how these prescriptions were to be understood by Jesus' disciples.[22] Prayer was to mean not just private prayer but also the keeping of the commandments and praying in common. Fasting meant 'a wide asceticism demanded by living a life of joy; and alms-giving meant, among other things, justice as well as charity'.[23] Those with a healthy spirituality know, at some level, the call to holiness – that is, a call to live the 'life of the spirit' authentically and within the world of God's creating and recreating. These themes are revisited in Chapter six.

Imbalances, in the way that Rolheiser describes them, may not be hazardous in the short term and may be caused by circumstances beyond an individual's control. Failure to comply precisely with such prescriptions need not be regarded pejoratively but with the compassion of a loving

---

20. Athanasius, *Against the Arians*, discourse 1, paragraph 39. Public domain.
21. R. Rolheiser, *Seeking Spirituality*.
22. Matthew 6.
23. Rolheiser, 1998, p.51.

Lord in mind, one who has entered into human life and knows of its complexities and challenges. The key to following this prescription for discipleship lies as much in disposition as in execution, in wanting to keep these things in balance.

Dwellers all in time and space [24]

Our regenerate nature is set free of temporal restraint and our new reality is spatially oriented, but life is lived out in a temporal context, rooted in the ordinary and the everyday. It is characterised by eating, sleeping, washing, cleaning, travelling, waiting in line and so on, and yet none of these activities divorces us from spatial reality. Nouwen regards the everyday activity of 'waiting' as an opportunity to identify with the God who waits for us: a God not constrained by the temporal but who is happy to dwell in temporality with us. Nouwen takes us on from waiting as a chore to understanding waiting as an opportunity to offer a prayer, and further again to an appreciation of waiting as God-lived dwelling. [25]

Similarly, saying 'grace' before and after meals does more than give thanks for food or bring to mind the needs of others. The words of the grace and the prayerful disposition of the company give spatial contextuality to the temporality of eating. The words of the grace give prayerful expression to the spirituality of the ordinariness of eating. Here we have an example of the relationship between spirituality, temporality and spatiality as expressed in prayer. Spirituality in the ordinary is the root and branch of the contemplative tradition. It seems as though the more ordinary, human and temporal

---

24. From the hymn 'Praise, my soul, the King of heaven', words by H. F. Lyte (1793–1847), based on Psalm 103.
25. H. J. M. Nouwen (1995), *The Path of Waiting*, London: DLT.

the phenomenon, the more exciting the possibility of spatial encounter with the living God!

Integrated spirituality

I sense that we all know what integrated and authentic spirituality looks like. It is something we rarely see in ourselves but we see it in others. We may know people who seem to be 'altogether' – at one with God and the world around them. We may say they give us a glimpse of God in Christlike qualities and in the fruit of the Spirit.[26] Perhaps this is what we mean by holiness. Donald Nicholl, in his book entitled *Holiness*, describes holiness as 'a snare and a delusion unless it draws us to the Holy One.'[27] The spirituality of others is likewise a snare and a delusion if it does not draw us either to the God within them or point us to the God all around us. One thinks of such people as Mother Teresa of Calcutta (1910–1997), who exuded the holiness of God and pointed to the poor of the world as the dwelling place of God.

The supreme example of totally authentic and integrated spirituality is our Lord Jesus Christ, who models for us full humanity in which the fullness of God is pleased to dwell and whose deeply spiritual relationship with the Creator Father God is complemented by his deep love and concern for all creation. We must ever keep before us the model of Jesus. We are his disciples and we are shaped by his indwelling Spirit. The aim of every Christian soul is union with God in Christ and our aim, and our destiny, is to become like him.[28]

---

26. Galatians 5:22, 23.
27. D. Nicholl (1981), *Holiness*, London: DLT, p.viii.
28. 1 John 3:1-3.

We also have the example of the apostles, and of saints and martyrs in every generation. A study of them shows us the rich diversity of spirituality. We, like them, have a unique spirituality which is ever developing and being transformed by an ever-deepening relationship with God that manifests in a genuine love for others and a care for all creation. It is this deeply transforming interconnectedness that marks out the saints and marks us out too.

Among the many who might inspire us is one whose integrated and authentic spirituality, I believe, is worthy of a little reflection in this context. It is that of Mary, the mother of Jesus.

Mary's story

Mary offers an example of integrated and authentic Christian spirituality. All that happened to her, both through the powerful action of God and through joyful, sorrowful and glorious life events, shaped the person she became; they shaped her spirituality. Mary was conditioned by her early nurture in faith and religious practice and she would have formed her own mental image of God, her own constructs of God (her theology) that would have been informed by what she had been taught, by what was held in common by her people and by what she had personally experienced.

The Bible tells us precious little about Mary, but legend has it that the evangelist Luke drew some of his narrative from her accounts of the birth and childhood of Jesus. Among those accounts we have the story of the visit of the angel Gabriel to Mary, the awesome Annunciation of the Lord, when Mary received the invitation to welcome into her body the incarnate Word of God. Durrwell asserts that early Christian theologians had a saying that 'Mary conceived in her soul before conceiving in her body.'[29]

Conception and birth are the first life events to happen to us. In addition, when we become Christians we experience rebirth as we invite God's Spirit to dwell in us. It is our *fiat* to conceiving the life of God in us and through us to the world. This is not to deny God's presence in all his creation. Far from it. The handprint of the Creator is imprinted on the creation, but welcoming Christ into our life is a seminal moment. There are other seminal moments in life when we rediscover God, perhaps having drifted and having found ourselves at some distance from God. Perhaps there have been other moments, such as when we have gained fresh insights or experienced breathtaking moments of mountaintop revelation. (I call them 'Aha!' moments!) Paradoxically, we discover something of God, too, in moments of deep sorrow, pain, hurt, anguish or despair. In many circumstances we reach for the God deep inside us and for the God out there, all around us. We may know times of consolation and of desolation, times when God seems near and times when God seems tantalisingly just out of reach, and times when we have found God sitting with us in life's mess.

Vignettes of Mary's life, as described in Scripture, show how much she is like us in this respect. God the Life of the world was born in Mary. We might ponder on how she might have felt when Joseph, her betrothed husband, needed persuading that the child she carried was from God. Then there is Mary perplexed by the words and actions of her 12-year-old son, and the wonder at the miracles performed by his hand. Mary was not the first or the last mother to witness

---

29. F. X. Durrwell (1990), *Mary: Icon of the Spirit and of the Church*, Slough: St Paul Publications, p.51.

the public execution of her son. Tradition has it that Mary was among the host of disciples who experienced the power of the Holy Spirit on the Day of Pentecost. Life happened to Mary! Through our participation in God's mission of love, we give birth to the Saviour as we manifest his presence in the fruit of the Spirit. He is to be found in the fruit we bear in love, joy, peace, patience, kindness, generosity, faithfulness, gentleness and self-control.[30]

Our spirituality, like that of Mary and of countless other witnesses, is shaped by our life in God: by the life-shaping Spirit of God within us and by God's presence and action in those we encounter, as well as by life-shaping events and experiences. Our spirituality is the heart of us because that is where we find God. We are enveloped, too, along with all creation, in the vast heart of the Father's love made manifest in the enfleshed love of God in Jesus and present to all in the Holy Spirit.

We will return to this theme in Chapter five, but for the purpose of this reflection we need only hold to the centrality of our spirituality as being the 'heart' of who we are. Durrwell asserts that:

> in the language of the Bible 'the heart' is the inmost depths of a person where communion is established with God, where the intelligence and the will find they are undivided and from where thoughts and feelings arise; where free decisions are worked out. Mary for her part speaks of her 'soul [which] magnifies the Lord'. The word means at one and the same time the being in its depths and the entire person.[31, 32]

30. Galatians 5:22, 23.
31. Durwell, *Mary: Icon of the Spirit and of the Church*, p.48.
32. Luke 1:46.

Christian spirituality experienced and expressed

Spirituality is not something we do, and yet to express our spirituality we find that we use words, postures or gestures, prayer practices, activities or disciplines to help us to express the inexpressible and articulate the inarticulable. We may have images of God – either conjured from our imagination or the imagination of others in biblical descriptions or through the skill of artists and craftsmen – and these might aid devotion or they might inhibit it. Conversely, images of God may have coloured our theological perspective rather than being iconographical of our theology or spirituality.

What else speaks to us of God and what resonates with the life in us that we call our spirituality? Perhaps it is a glorious sunset, a warm bath, a lover's embrace. Perhaps it is the soaring music of Byrd or Mozart. (Hans Küng and Karl Barth would agree with that!) Perhaps it is the cry of a newborn baby. We have demonstrated over many centuries that we have a very human need to explicate and to incarnate the mystical. We need also to recognise the spiritual in the incarnated.

Our religious practices, our preferred style of public worship and personal devotion are responses to God, but they also derive from God, with the Holy Spirit igniting or eliciting devotion. We are drawn to expressions of our God-relationship. It is Love that draws us to worship. It is simply (and profoundly) the love of God for us. We are drawn to love God back. We were created by God and gifted with God-life. We belong in God, and responding to God through the conduit of worship demonstrates that belonging. It is an acknowledgement of our true identity and our true home.

As we go through life we are loved and nurtured or buffeted and bashed by life events and human relationships.

The humanity in us seeks God; it cries out to God in deep sighs and longing for God-given expression in a variety of forms. As the hymn has it:

> As pants the hart for cooling streams
> when heated by the chase,
> so longs my soul, O God, for thee
> and thy refreshing grace.[33]

The words of the hymn are based on Psalm 42. The psalms have ever been a rich source of devotional expression and 'speak' to us in a range of human circumstances and moods.

Sometimes worship and prayer practices are rooted not so much in conscious desire as in conscience-related dutiful response to God who is to be worshipped and honoured. At other times they are barely expressed: times and occasions of profound being whilst doing little except sustaining a receptive disposition as we allow God's gaze to bathe us, as we gaze back in awe and wonder. Sometimes our worship and devotional practices are the expression of exuberance and joy, profound sorrow or regret or heartfelt gratitude. Sometimes they focus on bringing before God the needs of others, as we express our deepest desires for the coming of God's kingdom of love with justice and equity for all.

If our public worship and personal devotional practices are to have integrity, they will express who we are, who we have become. The much quoted 'Pray as you can and not as you can't'[34] may bring, initially, a sense of relief, but on further reflection we may find that prayer resources that no longer work have not been replaced with new ones: the 'can't' of prayer, over a period of time, is spiritually debilitating and

---

33. N. Tate and N. Brady (1696), 'As pants the hart for cooling streams'. Public domain.
34. J. Chapman, OSB, Abbot of Downside (1938), *Spiritual letters* (1938) London: Sheed and Ward.

the 'can' of prayer does not really satisfy either! It is possible that the mechanistic repetition of familiar prayers has replaced life-giving and meaningful prayer. Prayers no longer express what we need or desire to express because they no longer reflect whom we have become. This is when we may need help, advice or permission to jettison what no longer works and to find eager anticipation and joy in exploring an adventure playground of tried and tested styles of worship or personal devotional practices that have been inspirational and helpful to others, and which might just work for us now.

As we delve into treasure chests of spirituality riches and examine treasures older and newer, we discover how relational devotion, as expressive of spirituality, might now resonate for those seeking a richer and deeper relationship with God and commensurate authentic expression of whom we are becoming.

CHAPTER TWO

Making sense of the journey

The Christian life is often referred to as a 'journey'. Unfortunately the word 'journey' has been overworked in recent times, but it does still suggest movement and a changing landscape, diversions and cul-de-sacs, and so it may resonate with the reader. I have chosen, therefore, to face the journey word head on!

Journeys can be exciting and full of adventure, but they can also be tedious, boring and predictable. Some journeys are undertaken reluctantly, against one's will; others are full of fear and anxiety about what will be experienced at journey's end. 'Journey' may not be a helpful metaphor for everyone, but it can open up discussion about life experienced, dreaded or anticipated. If nothing more, the 'journey' word sets us in time and space and helps us to acknowledge a past, a history and a future – an unknown.

The story of the journey may offer us an articulation in response to the question, 'Where have you come from, where are you going and how are you feeling right now?' Relate these questions to our journey in faith and we can open up a discussion about our relationship with God, with other people and with the environment in which we find ourselves. The question moves from 'Tell me about your journey in faith' to 'Introduce me to your God.'

What we understand God to be like is coloured by our experience of life. Further, our understanding of God at a given time, and in a given circumstance, may depend upon life circumstances. Alternatively, there may be a dissonance between an inherited or conditioned understanding of God and the contextuality of our life. For example, a taught or inherited belief in a wrathful or vengeful God may be unhelpful as we seek a God of mercy and compassion.

The way we relate to God – our theology – shapes the expression and articulation of our spirituality in prayer and worship. We may hold that what has been part of our spiritual and prayerful daily 'commute' has become less helpful, even meaningless, and that we are in need of encouragement or permission to explore other avenues or to stop off for a while at a 'station' to which we feel drawn or which intrigues us. We may need permission to say, 'I used to think God is like this but now I think God is like that, and now I feel drawn to engage with God or to worship God in a different way.' This chapter is about making sense of the journey and, if we are stuck somewhere in a spiritual or theological siding, about finding the resources to move on.

But what happens when desire ceases, appetite wanes, prayer brings no consolation, and we feel we are disintegrating? Perhaps we have ground to a halt. We are stuck! We may be able to see the way ahead but we seem rooted where we are. Conversely, we may have no vista at all and we may have become disoriented or stunned. We may be 'stuck' for other reasons too. Guilt, fear, resentment and not wanting to catch sight of God's loving gaze upon us can cause us to be stuck. We cannot move on because we cannot face the 'elephant' in the soul! To move on we may need to revisit familiar and life-giving 'stations' so that we can reinhabit relational echoes, out of necessity, safety or sentiment, or so that we can recall times of consolation.

In this chapter we will consider the signs and symptoms of being spiritually stuck: the reasons for a loss of appetite for what has previously fed us – for example, Scripture, prayer or liturgy. We will reflect on the possible Godgivenness of being 'stuck' and how God meets us in the mire. We will reflect, too, on how being stuck is also about being held, and we will think about what the Passion of Christ can teach us about being held against our will.

Static but not stuck!

Overheard on a bus journey: 'Are you having a holiday this year?'

'Yes, we're going down to the static for a couple of weeks.'

As the conversation unfolds it is revealed that one of the passengers has a mobile home that is permanently sited on the East coast. The permanently sited mobile home has wheels which never turn. It is mobile yet static.

Life is full of contradictions, and our spiritual life is no exception. As we have already observed, our spiritual life cannot be separated from the rest of our life or from the lives of those around us. The conversation overhead on that bus journey reveals something of what is important to my fellow passengers: how they balance work and recreation; how they live. That busload of passengers are sharing a journey. There may be much else that they share but they may never know the detail of it. For now, strangers as they are to one another (for the most part), they share a common goal in terms of the direction of the bus, until they alight at different points to continue their journeying by other means.

Although the word 'journey' is somewhat overworked, there would seem to be no avoiding its metaphorical use. In this chapter we consider journeying in spiritual and theological terms, and we also consider the value of being static. We will distinguish stasis from being stuck in the way that John, the character in the previous chapter, described himself as being stuck.

May we reflect a little longer on the non-mobile home on the East coast? By all accounts, the home on wheels was not stuck in its present position. The owners liked where it was sited. It suited their purposes because, whilst it gave them freedom from where they lived for most of the year, it also offered familiarity. The owner described to her friend how convenient it was – near the site shop but not too near, a short walk to the seashore but protected from the wind by Marram grass-covered dunes. The owners could 'pop down of a weekend' and within ten minutes could relax into the space it provided. They knew that, if they wanted a change, they could resite the home, but the current arrangement suited them well at that particular time in their life. In a world that urges us to move on, to move upwards in social status or in acquisitional terms, or to move on in relational terms, stasis is so easily undervalued.

In the early centuries of the Church's history, some Christian women and men took to the desert in their own version of the static caravan. The Desert Mothers and Fathers have left us with a beautiful legacy and a model of living the static life without being stuck. It would seem that two strong threads of thought became twined together in those centuries. The first is the belief that the Living God is to be found in the Holy Scriptures, and the second is that, thanks to the death and resurrection of Jesus and to the sending of the Holy Spirit at Pentecost, union with God, in the cosmic Christ, is possible this side of heaven.

To engage with Scripture, especially the Holy Gospels, is to foster that union with God in Christ: something which is at the heart of Christian discipleship. It characterises the first and most essential journey for any Christian – that is, the journey into the vast heart of the Father's love, by the power of the Holy Spirit and in union with Christ. This is the journey we are all on, but the Desert Fathers and Mothers lived a static life; for the most part, each in their own 'static'. It was largely a hermetical, anchorite life. Their journeying was deeply spiritual rather than physical, though aceticism, self-denial and fasting were considered necessary for greater concentration on the essential work of prayer.

The work of prayer (*opus Dei*) established and settled by the Desert Mothers and Fathers was foundational to the development of monasticism and to a way of prayerfully engaging with God in the Holy Scriptures. This deep engagement or 'chewing' of the Holy Scriptures became known as *Lectio Divina*: a slow, contemplative praying of the Scriptures which enables the Bible, the word of God, to become a means of union with God. It is a way of praying Scripture (and other material) through study, allowing us to ponder, listen, pray and sing within the soul. This devout method of engagement would be practised for several hours each day. We may not have that facility but we may be attracted to the idea of deep engagement with God, and we have free access to the Holy Scriptures.

Lectio Divina, sometimes referred to as 'Holy Reading', is enjoying something of a resurgence of popular appeal. Those readers who are familiar with *Lectio Divina* may wish to skip the next few paragraphs. Those who may be intrigued by it might find the following helpful. Authorities on *Lectio Divina* advocate, as St Benedict did, four phases (sometimes called 'feasts'). I suggest that for *Lectio* to be more beneficial, the four phases need to be framed with an initial time of preparation and a time of review afterwards: that is six phases in all. The following is a brief summary of each phase:

1. Preparation

First we choose a place for this encounter with God, preferably a place where we shall not be disturbed. A place where we can read out loud is ideal.

Time spent with God by engaging with the Holy Scriptures is never a waste of time! Most of us would say that we have so much to do that we don't have a lot of time. The wonder of *Lectio* is that one can engage with the process for as little or much time as one can manage. So the first decision to make is how long we can give to it on this occasion. This will, to some extent, determine how long we can spend in each phase. It is imperative, however, that we don't skip any one phase altogether.

Having decided how long we can spend (15 to 30 minutes might be long enough for those who are new to it), we then consider where we are with God, where we are in our relationships with the people in our life, and with the world in general. Here we note our mood. Next we call to mind God's presence and ask God to open the ears of our heart. Here the prologue of the Rule of St Benedict might be helpful:

> Listen, O my son, to the precepts of thy master, and *incline the ear of thy heart*, and cheerfully receive and faithfully execute the admonitions of thy loving Father, that by the toil of obedience thou mayest return to Him from whom by the sloth of disobedience thou hast gone away.[35]

We are preparing to be static before God for the allotted period of time with the intention of being still long enough

---

35. T. Fry (ed) (1981), *The Rule of St Benedict*, Minnesota: The Liturgical Press, p.15.

to be able to hear the voice of God. If we currently feel 'stuck', we might pray that through this encounter with God we may become a little less stuck. We adopt a disposition of openness to the possibility of encounter with God, approaching this time with eager anticipation.

2. Reading the text

Now we read the text we have chosen. The reader may ask how one decides which text to read. Perhaps you are following a Bible reading scheme or perhaps you plan to take one book of the Bible (maybe one of the Gospels) and read through it a little at a time. You may prefer to open the Bible at a random page and engage with the text before you. My experience is that no particular method is necessarily better than any other. God can speak through whatever we choose, but part of our listening to God in preparation for this time is to listen for inspiration as to where in Scripture to engage. I would suggest, however, that generally 'less is more': a short passage of Scripture allows for in-depth reflection.

The next step may feel counter intuitive in these days of rapid absorption of information. Read the passage slowly, noting any words or phrases that stand out. Read the passage several times, out loud if possible. Hear yourself articulate the precious word of God as you 'chew it' over and over again.

3. Meditation (*Meditatio*)

Here we ponder on the passage we have just read, benefiting from the illumination given by God's Holy Spirit. There is nothing wrong here with examining the passage exegetically, bringing to it everything you know about it – who wrote it and why, and who it was written for. If you are using a Bible commentary, this is the time to refer to anything that helps to deepen your understanding of the passage. This phase is about engaging with the brain.

4. Prayer (of Consecration) (*Oratio*)

Here we allow God to touch and to heal us through the word he has given. Just as Holy Communion changes us, so does this communion with God in Holy Scripture. We engage our heart and dwell on our heartfelt gratitude to God for this time and for the illumination the Spirit has given us. It may be that the passage has highlighted an area of our life that needs attention, or maybe we have been challenged in other ways. We thank God for grace, mercy and love freely given. From deep within us we articulate our gratitude and our resolve to love and serve God better.

5. Contemplation (*Contemplatio*)

Finally we allow words to fail us and we sink into a time of resting in the presence of God. Contemplation is a simple, loving focus on God, a joyful rest in the presence of the One who loves us. If time is running short, do not skip this phase; rather truncate all the phases so that you still arrive at this point, albeit briefly.

This phase ends in resolution. How am I to live following this encounter with God? It is time to plan for action. Action and contemplation are not different forms of praying but a gentle oscillation back and forth between spiritual 'activity' with regard to God and 'receptivity'. The move from being to doing and back again will, with practice, become seamless, effortless.

6. Reappraisal

Here we ask ourselves a series of questions. We call to mind our mood when we began the process and compare it with our mood now. How am I with God at the end of this time? How do I feel about the problems or challenges that remain before me? How do I feel, having had this short time of stasis? Do I feel less stuck? What action do I need to take?

The process of *Lectio Divina* is one of drawing closer to God (in order that God may draw closer to us) that we might become more Christlike and thereby be a more faithful (closer) image to Christ in helping him to bring in his kingdom.

Is *Lectio Divina* for everyone? I think so, but those not naturally drawn to reflection may have more difficulty with the discipline of it. Pragmatists might want to ask, 'How will this help to promote the good news of Jesus Christ? How can I afford to give time to this on top of everything else?' My response would be, 'Can you afford not to?' Remember the first commandment as well as the second! And remember: 'All scripture is inspired by God and is useful for teaching, for reproof, for correction, and for training in righteousness, so that everyone who belongs to God may be proficient, equipped for every good work.'[36] Study and reflection on, and praying through, Holy Scripture is a means of grace that can change us and restore in us the image and likeness of God. Once we discover the value of encountering God in Holy Scripture we can more easily empathise with the life choices of those early Christians.

Brother Andrew on *Lectio Divina*

Brother Andrew, married with a family and a Benedictine oblate, described what *Lectio Divina* means to him. He said that he regards *Lectio* as his main form of Bible study.

---

36. 2 Timothy 3:16-17.

I think Benedictines use *Lectio* in a variety of ways. My own approach is to set aside time for a short but fairly concentrated period of meditation, where I will let the Holy Spirit lead me to a particular word or phrase which I will then repeat slowly, chewing it over, for several minutes, before moving into intercession and then finally silence (contemplation). I have also developed what I call a process of 'extended *Lectio*,' where the process might last over the course of an entire day and where the word or phrase is revisited on several occasions, perhaps when I am out walking the dog, for example. *Lectio* simplifies complex texts, allowing me to really focus solely on what I perceive the Spirit to be saying. *Lectio* is not a panacea, however; some days it just doesn't seem to work and there is an inherent danger in seeking meditative purity. On days where nothing seems to chime my advice is just let it go; that might be all God requires of you for the moment in any case! On other occasions *Lectio* can take me to somewhere new and challenging, and I suspect that it is the fallow days that prepare me for the days of explicit spiritual intensity.

Imaginative contemplation

The reader might like to compare *Lectio Divina* from the Benedictine tradition with a way of engaging with God (especially with Jesus) from the Ignatian tradition. The process of 'Imaginative contemplation' is similar in some ways. Preparation with anticipation is still important. Reflecting on the chosen passage from the Holy Scriptures (especially the Gospels) focuses not so much on the exegesis of the passage as on allowing it to inform the imagination and all the senses, as one places oneself in the scenario. We imagine what Jesus might say to *us* in that scenario, and we prayerfully respond. Reflection on the encounter with the

Lord during the contemplation and resolutions for living more faithfully conclude the process.

Close encounters with God

I would encourage the reader to take a few minutes to reflect and, if you will, to imagine yourself back in the fifth century AD. Perhaps you are a recent convert to Christianity. Perhaps you are a second-, third- or fourth-generation Christian. You have taken the message of the gospel seriously. Christ is central to your life. You want to follow him, to live as he would have you live; but, more than that, you hear in the Scriptures and in the teaching of the Church that union with Christ is possible this side of heaven. But what does the wisdom of the age teach you about how best to live as a faithful disciple of Jesus Christ? How much depends on you, and how much depends on the grace of God? You know yourself well enough to know what appetites, what inclinations, what predilective sins beset you. What do other serious-minded Christians do when they want to follow Christ so closely? What lifestyle do they adopt in order to live a holy life? What characterises it? Prayer, fasting, self-denial, celibacy, study, gainful employment (the devil gives work to idle hands!)? How reasonable, how realistic is it?

Not everyone is called to be a hermit, though most of us would like a little time alone now and again! For the most part we live in community. In fact, we live in more than one community. There is the community of our home and family, and of our extended family. There may be the community of our workplace, school or college. There may be the community of hobbies and interests: the gym, the reading group, the bingo club.

The emergence of living in community in order to seek God together with others and to be tested and challenged in living a grace-filled life signified a watershed in the developing life of the Christian Church, but to say it was a new idea would be completely erroneous. We have the example of the common life led by Jesus and the 12 disciples. We have insights into early Church communities through the New Testament epistles. It may be too crude a distinction to make, but the question for the Desert Mothers and Fathers was not about conversion or about how to make disciples of all nations, but how to live faithfully the Christian calling to union with God in Christ: to perfection (better translated from the Greek as 'completion') and to virtuous living. This was to be achieved by avoiding temptation and distraction. Any anchorite will say, however, that spending time alone with God removes neither temptation nor distraction! Being confronted with one's own self is hugely challenging.

Here we consider a way of growing in grace, and one which more closely resembles the way most of us live – that is, with other people. On the smorgasbord of spirituality savouries offered in this book as 'tasters', we consider the spirit of Benedictinism.

In the fifth century AD came one Benedict of Nursia (c.480–c.550) who was responsible for developing a monastic tradition in the West, and about whom little is known. Such knowledge as we have about the life of St Benedict comes mostly from the writings of St Gregory (540–604). Benedict has been called the Father of Western monasticism, though this has been challenged in recent decades. Some authorities point to the monk Cassian, a contemporary of Benedict, and argue that his long-winded rule for living a Christocentric life was a valuable source that

Benedict used in the writing of his Rule. Until the last century, scholars thought that Cassian had adapted Benedict's rule. In any case, at that time there was a body of wisdom around the Christian world that had developed since the earliest days of Christendom about how to live a truly faithful and holy Christocentric life. For the source of Benedict's guidance we should, therefore, include the wisdom of the Desert Fathers and Mothers, Cassian and the anonymous 'Rule of the Master'.

The key question then: How can we live faithfully the Christian life? For 1500 years, Benedict's legacy to the Church has enabled countless Christians to live a Christocentric, grace-filled life, and one of the key characteristics of Benedictine spirituality is the importance of being static. Benedictine monks and nuns take a vow of stability (*stabilitas*) – a lifelong commitment to stay with the same community and the same abbey. Benedict's description in his Rule of different kinds of monks highlights the value he places on stability. His language is sharp and uncompromising:

First, there are the cenobites, that is to say, those who belong to a monastery, where they serve under a rule and an abbot.

Second, there are the anchorites or hermits, who have come through the test of living in a monastery for a long time, and have passed beyond the first fervour of monastic life. Thanks to the help and guidance of many, they are now trained to fight against the devil. They have built up their strength and go from the battle line in the ranks of their brothers to the single combat of the desert. Self-reliant now, without the support of another, they are ready with God's help to grapple single-handed with the vices of body and mind.

Third, there are the sarabaites, the most detestable kind of monks, who with no experience to guide them, no rule to try them *as gold is tried in a furnace*[37], have a character as soft as lead. Still loyal to the world by their actions, they clearly lie to God by their tonsure. Two or three together, or even alone, without a shepherd, they pen themselves up in their own sheepfolds, not the Lord's. Their law is what they like to do, whatever strikes their fancy. Anything they believe in and choose, they call holy; anything they dislike, they consider forbidden.

Fourth and finally, there are the monks called gyrovagues, who spend their entire lives drifting from region to region, staying as guests for three or four days in different monasteries. Always on the move, they never settle down, and are slaves to their own wills and gross appetites. In every way they are worse than the sarabaites. It is better to keep silent than to speak of all these and their disgraceful way of life. Let us pass them by, then, and with the help of the Lord, proceed to draw up a plan for the strong kind, the cenobites.[38]

Perhaps the increase in popularity of Benedictinism in recent decades is due in part to the search in the human soul for stability in an increasingly mobile world. Social scientists, geographers and anthropologists describe how people these days are generally more likely to move away from their roots: to change homes, friends, spouse, life partner and more. Esther de Waal reminds us that Benedict's context was a 'troubled, torn apart, uncertain world . . . a world without landmarks':[39] this may be part of the appeal of Benedictinism in our own times.

St Benedict and his sister Scholastica, drawing on the experience of the Desert Mothers and Fathers, show the value, in terms of spiritual growth of stability, of stasis which causes

37. Proverbs 27:21.
38. T. Fry, *The Rule of St Benedict* RB 1.1–12.
39. E. De Waal (1999), *Seeking God: the Way of St Benedict*, Norwich: The Canterbury Press, p.1.

us to confront relational difficulties, to face the hard truth about ourselves and which fosters growth in the only true journey to which we are all called – the journey in which we seek and find the living God in the context of our fellow journeyers. The key question in the days of the Desert Fathers and Mothers and in the days of St Benedict was, 'How can we live faithfully the Christian life?' I suggest that the question in our hearts and minds today is no different, and that the answer is to be found as much in the ancient spirituality traditions of the Church as it is to be found in more contemporary spirituality expressions and practices.

Brother Andrew on Benedictine stability (*stabilitas*)

As an oblate, Brother Andrew is part of the extended community of a particular abbey. He said that this makes him

> consider what stability might mean for me as a 'Lay Benedictine.' My own take is that it means a lifelong commitment to a people, a practice and a place. The group of people to whom I am most committed is my family, my wife and two daughters. The concept of stability has caused me to reflect on what it means to live as a married Christian and I definitely regard my marriage as a form of religious community, nourished through an ongoing commitment to shared spiritual practices including the saying of an office a day with my wife; the saying of grace together before meals, participation in the life and worship of the parish church and so on. Shared recreational activities, walking the dog, going to rugby matches etc. is also part of our life together, and I would be cautious of demarcating too rigidly the distinction between the sacred and the secular. Finally, commitment to place covers how we use the house to serve the needs of others as well as ourselves and ministry within the parish.

I asked Brother Andrew what had initially attracted him to Benedictine spirituality. He replied that it was because it offered a new way of not only thinking about his faith but also living out his faith. The idea of community had always been important to him, and Benedictine spirituality is at heart a communal spirituality, where each person's spiritual growth is dependent on others who are also undertaking a similar journey. He described how Benedictine practice, with its focus on hospitality, resonates strongly with his family understanding of what it means to be 'property-owning Christians in the world'. By this I understood him to mean that what God has provided is to be used for the benefit of visitors and strangers; this is an important aspect of Benedictine spirituality. Brother Andrew attested to the importance, for him, of the vow which is a pledge to try to live, by the grace of God, a Christlike life. The balance of corporate worship and personal prayer and the fact that St Benedict's Rule is 'soaked in Scripture' also has great appeal to him.

Brother Andrew models his family life according to Benedictine principles. Today a number of communities comprising families and single people are living in a similar manner. This (so-called) 'New Monasticism' is characterised by holding all property in common and living a wholesome lifestyle with mutual accountability.

Spiritual roadblocks: not static – just stuck!

No one is called to be stuck, though we may be stopped in our tracks by God – perhaps like St Paul on the Damascus Road,[40] although with considerably less light intensity! If we

---

40. Acts 9:1-19.

are stopped in our tracks we do need to consider what purpose God has in it. We may be halted by life events, things that not only take us 'off course' but also 'derail' us, leaving us dazed and disoriented. We consider these further in Chapter four. Here we consider what it is like to feel stuck in our spiritual life in the way that John announced to his spiritual director in Chapter one.

Being stuck can be about many different things, and it may take time to get to the heart of the problem. It can be variously described, for example, as not being able to see the way ahead ('My prayer life is not getting me anywhere', 'My habit(s) of sin remain(s) unchanged despite my best efforts', 'I am not growing spiritually'). Such concerns may be too rooted in a very human drivenness to make progress. But how are we to measure? We may, of course, be trying to measure up to the stature of the fullness of Christ. The writings of St Paul are shot through with earnest imploring to live a better life, a life more worthy of our calling. The problem is that some people are prone to hyperscrupulosity, and the effort to live a grace-filled and virtuous life can be so pathologically damaging that life is devastated, even taken away altogether.

Getting to the root of the problem

At the centre of many of us is what has been described as 'oughtitis' or 'a hardening of the oughtries'. It is responsible for the number of times we believe we must or should do something. It is a driver that goes far beyond that of the duty of a Christian towards God or humankind. Perhaps, as layers are peeled back, it might be discovered that the root of the problem is something about not truly believing that God loves us just the way we are, that God loves us infinitely and that makes us infinitely loveable. It may be that the problem lies in not loving ourselves the way we are, in not making friends with ourselves in a way that allows us to forgive ourselves or to make allowances for ourselves. There is a healthy balance to be struck that keeps us gently striving to be faithful without damaging God-given goodness in us.

Being spiritually stuck can be rooted in serious sin. It is the kind of stuck we can be when we try to avoid someone's gaze. In this instance it is God's loving gaze that transfixes us! There seems to be nowhere else to look. Eventually the gaze becomes unavoidable. We are stuck for choices of where else to look! 'Is there something seriously amiss between me and God at this time?' can be a useful question to ask ourselves. When asked that question by a spiritual guide we might feel affronted and respond indignantly, protesting our innocence. The guide can take that. The question is worth asking, though, because separation (in our own minds) because of sin can be very disabling and can, quite often, be put right through confession and the assurance of God's absolution.

Avoiding God

A third way of experiencing being stuck is somewhat related to the second. It is also about avoiding eye contact with God. In this instance, however, it is not about sin but about avoiding eye contact with God in case we are being called to do something. What might we be avoiding? I am privileged to hear many stories of vocational journeys, and in many people's experience there has been an element of not wanting to catch God's eye, of avoiding the subject because to engage with God might mean having to make lifestyle changes or make sacrifices.

Seeking satisfaction in worship and prayer

A fourth description of being stuck comes from unrealistic expectations, especially in public worship or private prayer. The absence of spine-tingling, mountaintop experiences is interpreted by some Christians as either the absence of God or the failure of worship to inspire or satisfy. For prayer to be effective it does not have to be affective. Its primary purpose is to worship God: to honour, praise, show gratitude, bring petition, if you will. Its primary purpose is not to give the worshipper a cosy glow or an adrenalin rush. Biographies of St Teresa of Avila, as well as her own writings, describe how for more than two decades she felt nothing in prayer. Then one day she burst into tears in front of a crucifix and, renewed in spirit, set about reforming the whole of the Carmelite order! Sometimes prayer is a matter of keeping the appointment with God even if nothing seems to be happening. Worship of 'The Other' is precisely that – The Other and not me!

How kind God is! God knows that we cannot easily keep turning up for worship unless our mind and our senses are fed from time to time. Liturgy, ritual, colour, music, bread, wine and incense all have their place in Christian worship. What gives us a spiritual boost depends on the sort of person we are, and the culture in which we live or in which our faith has been nurtured. Such sensual experiences as come our way in worship are, however, more safely considered a gift, a bonus, than a right.

Perseverance and obedience

In spite of St Teresa's stoic example of faithfulness, it can be right for some to move on to another place of worship, to another corner of the Lord's vineyard to sample something new or different from among the rich heritage of the worldwide Church. In the short term it may be a matter of staying close to God through perseverance. It brings to mind the 1974 version of the movie *The Karate Kid* in which a young man seeks the help of a karate expert to help him to face up to bullies. Mr Miyagi, the karate teacher, has the young man wax and polish cars for several weeks. The young man cannot see how this is helping him to learn karate until Mr Miyagi demonstrates how 'Wax on, wax off' is building self-control and essential muscular strength. In my role as chaplain of a seminary I find myself whispering, 'Wax on, wax off' to women and men training for the priesthood when they are looking somewhat downhearted as they emerge from Morning Prayer on a cold winter day! Obedience is a key word here: key, but not always popular!

Responding actively or passively to being 'stuck'

When we are spiritually stuck we tend to assume that we must do something about it. Doing something seems better than doing nothing. We live in a world that values activity over passivity. It has been thus since the creeping influence of Greek philosophy on the early Church. But it was not always so, and it was not so for Jesus. There is another perspective, and it is sobering for those hooked on activity. It is that the world was saved not by activity but by passivity.

The Gospels show a marked change from activity to passivity, action to passion, at the point where Jesus was 'handed over' in the Garden of Gethsemane. William Vanstone, the great twentieth-century priest and writer, devotes the whole of the second half of his book, *The Stature of Waiting*, to what he describes as the passivity of Jesus, a word he reminds us has the same root as the word 'passion'.[41] He

41. W. H. Vanstone (1982), *The Stature of Waiting*, London: DLT.

describes in detail how, from the time that Jesus is handed over in the Garden of Gethsemane to his death on the cross, he is passive; he allows his tormentors, his torturers, his murderers to do what they will. For Vanstone, it is in Jesus' passivity (in his passion) and not in his actions that he saves the world. Jesus voluntarily gives up all power to act. He does not call down cosmic forces to destroy his enemies. He does not miraculously descend from the cross unscathed. He freely gives. He gives himself up to whatever will happen next. This fully human Jesus could not know, any more than we could, the final outcome. This is complete abandonment. This is total risk-filled vulnerability.

Letting go in prayer, being passively obedient, can be very difficult, but letting go of the worry that we cannot pray can be amazingly fruitful and liberating. Once we let go of the idea that prayer is something we *do*, something we feel we should obtain something from, and realise that it is a 24-hour relationship we are *in*, a time of prayer becomes a time of conscious encounter with God. It is an encounter with the otherness of God that is beyond sensual satisfaction. The Other is God who is prepared to come to *us*, not just to meet us halfway. God comes to us not only when we are strong and able to put in boundless energy to make the relationship work; God comes when we have nothing to offer, when we are weary and drained of resources.

Allowing for change and growth

A fifth and final suggestion as to why we may be spiritually stuck is that we are trying to relate to God in ways that used to work but no longer work. There might be two reasons for this. The first is that our theology has changed: our understanding, knowledge and experience of God is not what it used to be. In simple terms, cardboard cut-out, two-dimensional images of God that were so helpful, comforting or frightening as a child bear no resemblance to how we now understand God to be. Secondly, our worship and devotional practices no longer express who we have become. We can no longer worship in a particular style with integrity and authenticity.

We will explore further what happens to shape who we have become, but for the purposes of this reflection on being stuck and how we might become unstuck, we might simply need permission to pray or worship in a different way. In one sense our Christian journey has been lifelong (it began before we were formed in the womb), but our conscious journeying into Christ may have begun when we were children, or it may have begun more recently. In either case it is possible that what served us well at our initial encounter with Church is no longer appropriate. It is time to try something different. My hope is that the reader may be encouraged to sample the riches of the Christian spirituality traditions, and so I offer a simple exercise to help identify whether the Holy Spirit is leading you towards a different way of relating to God than has been experienced thus far.

Mapping the journey

This exercise involves reflecting on what looks, at first glance, like a map of the London Underground system (see diagram opposite). The ever-loving triune God is central to every spiritual journey. Consider the spiritualities, worship and prayer styles that characterise the regular commute journeys of many Christians. Do you recognise your own commute? Reflect for a few moments on where you have travelled in

Prayer and spirituality – a 24-hour relationship with God

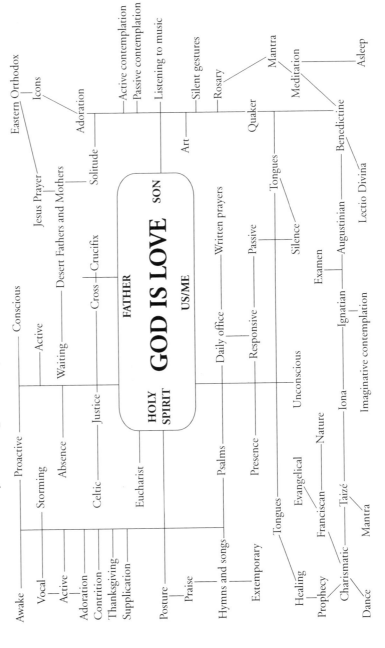

past times and what journeys serve you now. Draw a circle around 'stations' with which you are familiar.

Now let your eye wander to unfamiliar 'stations'. Which ones intrigue you? Which ones might you feel drawn towards? Perhaps you once found vocal prayer fulfilling but latterly you feel drawn to silence. Perhaps you once eschewed any kind of imagery in worship but now find yourself drawn to the iconographic tradition. Draw a line under the 'stations' to which you feel drawn and make a note to yourself to pursue them with an open mind and with a sense of adventure and expectation of a richer, fuller, closer relationship with God. Perhaps some stations are missing. Why not write them in? In which zone do they belong?

If our public worship and personal devotional practices are to have integrity, they will express who we are, who we have become. At the very least this exercise will be an appraisal of all that has gone before, and it may just ease our 'stuckness' enough to keep us going whilst we consider where we might next explore. Recalling once again that much-quoted epigram, 'Pray as you can and not as you can't',[42] might bring a pragmatism to our plight. Even if life is currently all about 'can't' rather than 'can', the very exercise of exploring new ways of relating to God in public worship and personal prayer demonstrates a desire to deepen our relationship and stay faithful to God. 'Can't' may become 'want to', and that may have to do for now! Be brave! Every one of the spirituality traditions, worship and prayer styles on this 'map' has nourished the spiritual lives of Christians at some time or another or in some part of the world. Between them they span more than 2000 years of experience of relating to the Christian God. There is something there for you at this time!

---

42. J. Chapman, *Spiritual Letters.*

Inward and outward journeying

Journeying in Christian spirituality has two axes. We speak of the 'inward journey' and of the 'outward journey'. Both lead to God. We all need to traverse both, though not necessarily at the same time. The inward journey leads to the discovery of God deep inside us, and the outward journey leads to the discovery of God in the world around us – in humankind and in all creation. If we invest everything in the inward journey we can become hopelessly self-centred rather than God-centred, and we can even persuade ourselves that they are one and the same. We can lose touch with God who is at work in the world and lose any incentive to meet God elsewhere and to work with God in the building of his kingdom. On the other hand, if we invest everything in the outward journey we can lose ourselves in feverish, albeit laudable, activity and persuade ourselves that all our activity, our exhaustion for Jesus, is a good thing. We lose our centre and can cease to hear the quiet voice of the divine Lover calling the Beloved to deep spiritual intimacy. There are times and seasons for the outward and the inward journeys and investments to be made in both. We need the guidance of the Holy Spirit to know where we are being led at any given time. This is a subject we will explore further in Chapters five and six.

We might want to distinguish here between journeying, which implies purposeful progression, and wandering, which implies no structure, route, map or compass. Both have a place in the history of God's people and in Christian spirituality. When God's ancient people were rescued from captivity in Egypt they seemed to begin a 40-year journey in the sense that we would like to hold it: a journey that taught them about God and his laws, that taught them about living together, and so much more. In reality it was 40 years of wandering! They knew where they had come from and there was, from time to time, a notion of the destination: the Promised Land. But between their starting and end points they often had no idea where they were, and they did not always trust Yahweh to show them the way or to keep them safe. Historians, tracing their itinerary, demonstrate meandering and doubling back. Little wonder the journey took 40 years! But was that such a bad thing? With hindsight we can see how God was at work among them and how *their* experience has enriched ours through the biblical accounts that give articulation to our own 'desert' wanderings. Someone who has never been lost can find it difficult to comprehend the terror of it. Perhaps you were once lost in a maze like the one at Hampton Court Palace. Of course, you might feel mild panic, but there would always be someone who would come along with whom you could share thoughts about the way out. If you shout loud enough, surely someone would come to the rescue? But when we are truly lost, there is no one to turn to, no way out – only despair and death. Sometimes spiritual growth comes out of first being completely lost.

A maze is a good example of how, at the heart, we need to be on the move. We can't stay still for long. From ancient times there have been carefully designed mazes or footpaths laid in intricate patterns to simulate journeying and its relationship to God. Labyrinths pre-date Christian times and they have different meanings in different cultures. They have been created to trap evil spirits or to lay out patterns for ritual dances. They have been designed to show the pathway mentioned at the beginning of this chapter: the one overarching journey each of us makes back to the vast heart of the Father's love, where the entrance of the maze or labyrinth indicates one's birth and God is depicted at the centre of it. In some extreme instances the labyrinth is a deity itself.

Non-Christian uses of labyrinths may discourage Christians from exploring the concept, but in Christian spirituality terms, labyrinths have been used as symbolic forms of pilgrimage: a journey or penance, perhaps, or a journey of enlightenment. In former times labyrinths became popular for those who could not afford to go on pilgrimage to the Holy Land or to other sites associated with Christian heritage. Pilgrimages remain popular, and other models of journeying can be found. For example, the devotion of 'The Stations of the Cross' is a form of pilgrimage in which Christ's journey to the cross and beyond is followed using Holy Scripture and artwork to engender devotion.

One can find mazes and labyrinths inside churches and in the grounds of monasteries and convents. They are used to foster contemplation and centring in prayer, the combination of progression and devotion modelling the spiritual journey. Processions do something similar. A modern day equivalent, popular among Christians, is the 'Prayer Walk' in either an urban or rural setting. Sights and sounds become the 'stations' that engender devotion or inspire prayer and reflection. Prayer walks are a good example of devotion that nourishes both the inward and the outward journeying in Christian discipleship and spirituality.

We end this chapter with a poem about journeying on which to reflect before we consider the effect that identity, self-awareness and personality have on spirituality.

The Journeyer

I paused to reflect and to study awhile
and Present asked where I had been.
I said I'd journeyed Inward
to places where each scene
told of faith and doubt;
of joy and sorrow
and everything in between.

Present asked me who I found there.
I answered readily,
'The Triune God: persons all three,'
for they had journeyed,
in death and life
and in glorious hue
they had come out to meet me!

She asked me who had shared my walk.
I thought of friends and family
but, too, those souls so good to me
like Ignatius, Benedict and Augustine, three
of many whose journey inward,
faithful and true,
had steered my course or cleared my view.

She asked me where else I had travelled.
I told her quite plainly
that I had travelled an Outward journey
to the edges and beyond and seen
views of fear and courage,
of love and pain,
and much else in between.

She asked me who I met there.
My reply was keen and strong:
I had met the Persons of the Triune God
on the edges and beyond;
for they had journeyed to meet me;
in the faces I had seen and
in the loving arms I'd been.

She wished me well as I journeyed on,
both Inward and Outward bound.
She rejoiced with me in all I'd seen
and in who's company I had found
the Triune God in persons three,
whom I had met and who met me
in whom unconditional love abound.

CHAPTER THREE

Spirituality, behaviour and personality type

This chapter is about Christian spirituality in relation to a dynamic, emergent human life becoming lived out and expressed in contextuality and mood. It is an exploration of the relationship between identity, personality and spirituality. In my experience, the question faced by many is, 'Who am I before God?' In part, the answer depends upon a degree of self-knowledge and self-awareness, although it also raises concerns about becoming self-absorbed, even self-obsessed. There is a need for balance: for honesty, for kindness and compassion towards oneself. As we search for our true identity (which is relational to both God and the world about us) we look for ways to assess who we are and in what ways we are changing shape.

As I develop my premise that spirituality in relation to personality is environmentally conditioned and subject to context, climate and mood, I would like the reader to consider how this affects a person's spirituality and the expression of it in prayer. My hope is that this will liberate us from being constrained by notions of being spatially or temporally fixed by stereotypical assessments of ourselves. At the same time we deepen our appreciation of how and why particular ways of relating to God are spatially and temporally conditioned or determined, but not fixed, and how to avoid being unhelpfully labelled or self-labelling.

Who am I?

No matter where we journey, we come sooner or later to be confronted by ourselves: who we are before God. Anthropologists suggest that a newborn baby, albeit briefly, resembles its father, and that this is vital if the father is to own paternity of the child and so protect and provide for it. Such authorities assert that this phenomenon is common within the animal world as a whole and is a legacy of human evolution. Creationists need not take offence at this point since we have the account in Genesis that humankind was created in the image and likeness of God. The implication here is that God recognises God-self in created order, and in humankind, and that we can recognise something of God in one another. The family of God's people have familial features and familial characteristics. Somewhere within that milieu of God and God's people is to be found our true identity.

We may want to argue that after creation came the Fall and that the image of God is marred in us: we are disfigured by sin. But disfigured is not the same as totally unrecognisable! God's view of us, based in pure and absolute love for us, is still that of God's image and likeness. God cannot create anything that is less than perfect; what we do with that creation, or what is done to us to mar it, is another matter. God's eye view of us is both created perfection and eschatological restoration. Is this not a better starting place than the more unhelpful and negative belief that we are not up to much, never have been and never will be? The words may vary but the sentiment is common enough among people. Perhaps Muriel's story will help our reflection.

Muriel's story

Muriel had never been a 'churchgoer'. She had seen people going in and out of her local church on a Sunday morning and had long since decided that church was not for the likes of her. She felt shabby just looking at their smart Sunday-best clothes as they came and went. Snatches of conversation overheard as she passed by on the way to the paper shop reinforced her view that the likes of her would not be welcomed. She couldn't 'talk proper'. She did believe in God but imagined God wouldn't want much to do with her either. She swore a lot, drank too much and had had, in her youth, a number of 'dalliances' with young men before she met and married Bert.

All this she shared with the vicar who came to see her after Bert died. Still numb from her sudden loss she didn't take in a lot of what he said, but he was kindly and gentle and didn't mind drinking tea from a mug. She tried to keep him in the front room but he followed her into the kitchen. She wished she had washed up the few dishes in the sink before he came. Without a pause in the conversation the vicar quietly washed up the few dishes, found the tea towel, dried the dishes and stacked them. Later, much later, Muriel would relate this incident to anyone who would listen. It was, for Muriel, the beginning of a long journey of discovery of her own worth and value and the realisation that she was loved and accepted by God.

It is not always God's view of us that we fear so much as the view other people have, which we might assume is more accurate than the view we have of ourselves. The poet Robert Burns left us with a shorthand note of this fear. In the final verse of his poem, *To a louse*, he writes:

auld scots (Lowland)

O wad some Pow'r the giftie gie us
to see oursels as others see us.
It wad frae monie a blunder free us
an' foolish notion.
What airs in dress an' gait wad lea'e us
an' ev'n Devotion.

which translates as:

modern english

Oh, that God would give us the very smallest of gifts
to be able to see ourselves as others see us.
It would save us from many mistakes
and foolish thoughts.
We would change the way we look and gesture
and to how and what we apply our time and attention.

Is that really true? It might be helpful if the way others see us is balanced and fair, but so often it is not. Moreover it is a snapshot. It is in a context because our behaviour is contextual. A funeral sometimes brings together people from different aspects of a deceased person's life: work colleagues, members of the bowling club, school friends, army comrades. Listening to conversations at the wake following the funeral, one hears accounts of the deceased's personality, habits, foibles, interests or sense of humour. So often mourners surprise one another with accounts of character traits, escapades or behaviour they do not recognise, eliciting declarations of, 'Well I never!' or 'I never knew that!'

We may find that people representing different dimensions of a person's life have different names for the deceased. William White might have been known at home as Bill, Dad or Granddad, but at work as Chalky or Gaffer. What is in a name? What does your preferred name say about you? Everyone who knows me knows that I hate my first name to be shortened to 'Ray' and that I have often threatened to have printed on a tee shirt: 'Shorten my name: shorten our friendship!' The reasons for disliking my name being shortened are not as important as my coming to the happy conclusion that my name is Raymond and that it says who I am *now*. No one but God knows all there is to know about us. No one but God can truly balance our virtues against our shortcomings, or can truly appraise our personality.

So often one hears people declare that if they were truly known by others they would not be liked, loved or accepted. Whatever life has thrown at them since babyhood, their self-image has been marred. Perhaps it was the emphasis on wrongdoing or failure to meet certain standards of behaviour or performance. Perhaps it was simply the absence of praise or recognition. Sometimes praise is not easily received; it is mistrusted, assumed to be mere flattery. Sometimes sincere praise is withheld for fear of causing another to be puffed up with pride. How careful we are to prevent others from committing the sin of pride! How proud we are to have done so! Is it not our experience that most people, most of the time, need encouragement to see themselves in a better light? Is it not the job of Christ our 'only mediator and advocate'[43] to present us to our Parent God in the best possible light? If the Church is to be the Body of Christ in the world, then our task, by the grace of the Holy Spirit, will include the work of restoration of image and likeness in ourselves and in one another, and of restoration of the creation God looked upon and called 'very good'. In practical terms, this means to fear pride less and to seek more opportunities to honour one another and to build one another up.

---

43. *The Book of Common Prayer* (first published 1662), From The Communion, prayer for the whole state of Christ's Church.

Psychological tools

Aids to understanding personality and behaviour in ourselves and in others have come in the form of psychological tools. Some have valued the work of social scientists in this exploration, in particular the field of psychology; from within that field some have found helpful tools which have their origin in the psychological research of the 1920s. It is not uncommon for someone to tell me that they have come to know themselves better using the language of psychological tools such as the Myers-Briggs Type Indicator (MBTI) or the Enneagram, which has its ancient origins in Sufism. Both MBTI and the Enneagram propound a dynamic of personality in the human aspiration for balance, roundedness and wholeness.

They may be fairly blunt instruments, but they have their uses, and they are becoming more and more popular in relation to spirituality because they can help us to identify why certain kinds of prayer practices or forms of worship do not draw us closer to God and do not aid our relationship with God, and why other ways might be worth trying.

There is no doubt that some find personality type labelling useful, not least as a starting point for further exploration; but there is a danger, having identified one's personality type, that one does not allow for change and growth in the way that is intended by trainers in the use of such psychological tools.

Works on this subject have much to recommend them. The works of Goldsmith and Wharton on spirituality and temperament,[44] Michael and Norrisey on prayer temperament

---

44. M. Goldsmith & M. Wharton (1993), *Knowing Me, Knowing You*, London: SPCK; M. Goldsmith (1994), *Knowing Me, Knowing God*, London: Triangle, SPCK.

in relation to the MBTI,[45] and Rohr and Ebert on *The Enneagram*[46] are particularly useful in raising awareness that personality type, evidenced and expressed in behavioural terms, is also contextual.

To this debate I bring the work of the American psychologist and feminist theorist William Moulton Marston (1893–1947), and a psychological framework that developed from his theories and was propounded in his monograph. Marston argues that, whatever our personality type, our behaviour will change according to the environment we are in. For example, if we move from a 'friendly' environment to a 'hostile' environment, we may become more or less confident or more or less inclined to trust or to listen.[47] My premise is that spirituality is, likewise, correlational and climatic. If we move to a mindset that God is hostile to us (rather than friendly), we will behave differently towards God, and this has potential consequences in spiritual and relational terms.

Public worship is also environmentally conditioned. Can you pray in church if you are too cold or too hot (rare indeed!)? If you are claustrophobic can you pray when a scrum of energetic Christians descend on you for prayer ministry? Perhaps you pray better on a beach than in a cathedral. Perhaps certain worship songs make you angry. In the previous chapter we considered how we may avoid God's gaze upon us, perhaps because of guilt or fear that God might ask something more of us. To that we could add that we might avoid God because we are in a bad mood!

45. C. P. Michael & M. C. Norrisey (1991), *Prayer and Temperament: Different Prayer Forms for Different Personality Types*, Charlottesville, The Open Door Inc

46. R. Rohr & A. Ebert (1990), *The Enneagram: A Christian Perspective*, New York: The Crossroad Publishing Company.

47. W. M. Marston (1928), *Emotions of Normal People*, London: Kegan Paul, Trench, Trübner & Co Ltd.

Our spirituality, and the expression of it in prayer, is not spatially or temporally fixed; it is contextual and conditional. To stay with the 'bad mood' example a little longer, we need to take note if we are very often in a bad mood and whether our bad mood is related to a certain context. The answer to our reflection may suggest changes we should make in our lifestyle, in how or where we worship, or in how we should approach correlated relational difficulties. Being honest with ourselves and bringing our bad mood before God may be the beginning of healing. The Psalms are invaluable in helping us to articulate our mood before God.

Jenny's favourite hymn

Jenny was asked, 'What is your favourite hymn?'

No particular hymn came to mind. After some thought she replied, 'It depends on the circumstance.' When asked to say more, she told the story of how she was walking home late one evening and found that there was no alternative to walking through a subway. As she walked, rather more briskly that usual, she sang the hymn, 'The King of love my shepherd is'. When asked if this was one of her favourite hymns, Jenny replied, 'Not really, but it got me through the subway!'

Under similar circumstances, what hymn might you sing? Compare that with walking away from an interview where you have been offered the job of your dreams. What hymn might you sing? The words of hymns contain a theological perspective, and spirituality is always based in theology. In this sense, mood has sought a theological framework and spiritual expression.

A closer look at the Myers-Briggs Type Indicator (MBTI)

Goldsmith and Wharton offer the following overview:

> According to Briggs and Myers there are sixteen different personality types; they are equally valid and each has its own particular strengths. No one type is more important than another. These sixteen types emerge by discovering where people fit on four distinct and separate scales, as a result of stating their preferences. It is important to recognise that *people place themselves*, and that the personality type which emerges is the one that seems to 'fit' the individual. There is no secret or sinister 'system' which reveals what people do not want to know or which classifies people against their will. The Type Indicator almost always reveals what people already know about themselves, but in a way which is structured and which enables them to understand and use the information creatively.[48]

According to Goldsmith and Wharton, Myers Briggs believed that there is a truly mutual usefulness of opposites and that we should value the differences of others and appreciate our own gifts. This, say the authors, 'more or less sums up the purpose of MBTI'.[49] MBTI is administered in the form of a questionnaire: responses to produce the score rating are on a scale of statements, in pairs; subjects choose which statement most closely reflects their own view of themselves. The outcome of the self-report questionnaire is a four-letter typology – for example, 'ESFJ', which is described by Goldsmith and Wharton as 'extroverted with sensing and feeling'.[50] A full expansion of the type indicated offers an account of how a person of a particular indicator might

---

48. M. Goldsmith & M. Wharton, *Knowing Me, Knowing You*, p.14.
49. Ibid, p.10.
50. Ibid, p.57.

think, behave, respond and react, and what they might need from themselves and from others in order to live a fulfilled life.

Christian writers expounding the value of the MBTI offer insights into which prayer practices, styles of worship and spirituality traditions are likely to resonate with particular personality types. In practice, I have witnessed numerous examples of people who, on discovering their MBTI and the correlated suggestions for spirituality and prayer, have shed the anxiety of years and have become unstuck from a time of deadness or dryness in prayer, worship or their relationship with God.

It can be argued that MBTI administered through a forced-choice questionnaire brings its own constraints, but in many psychometric tools there is an element of forced choice or a time constraint in application of the tool in order to avoid rumination getting in the way of deeper, instinctual reactions and responses.

A closer look at the Enneagram

The name comes from two Greek words, *ennea* meaning 'nine', and *gramma,* meaning 'sign' or 'figure'. The Enneagram is an ancient and dynamic typological model. Its use by Christians dates back several centuries. I heartily recommend Rohr & Ebert as the definitive Christian authority on the subject.[51] The Enneagram differentiates nine different characters, or personality types.[52] The authors claim that it 'shares with many other typologies the crude reduction of human behaviour to a limited number of character types'. Rohr relates how the Jesuits carefully studied the Enneagram and its origins before 'adopting it' as

---

51. R. Rohr & A. Ebert, *The Enneagram.*
52. Ibid, p.3.

a 'tool for spiritual counselling and as a model for retreat work'.[53] No scientific validation is offered but its adoption by Christian organisations of repute and by some psychological institutions in the USA is presented by the authors as sufficient justification for its use. Rohr says that

> it has been shown that the Enneagram is compatible with the Christian tradition of spiritual counselling and human leadership as well as with diverse psychotherapeutic approaches . . . but in the present state of affairs, the Enneagram does not claim to have been 'scientifically' corroborated.[54]

Although some might have concerns that the Enneagram has its roots in Eastern non-Christian mysticism, one hopes that if the likes of Richard Rohr espouse it there is no danger in its judicious adoption. Are we not all seekers after truth? Indeed, a reluctance to look beyond orthodox Christianity for something of truth can raise its own concerns. Rohr reminds us that 'the Enneagram was probably used for centuries to help spiritual directors train and refine the gift of "the reading of souls" (discernment) and the transforming of people into who they are in God.' So the authority of the Enneagram may come down to the notion that it has been used effectively within the Christian Church for a very long time. Much of Christian religious practice has its roots in other religions or philosophies, Jewish faith and practice being the most obvious. Many of our Christian traditions are rooted in paganism. Celtic spirituality, for example, owes much of its wholesome rootedness to philosophies and theologies of creation which cradled it. No Christian spirituality tradition is totally free of syncretism. In this, the Enneagram is no exception.

---

53. Ibid, p.20.
54. Ibid, p.20.

There is a danger of oversimplifying what is a sophisticated tool, but it is worth noting that the nine types identified, and numbered accordingly, are expressed as nine profiles of a personality. The nine types are labelled as:

1. The Perfectionist
2. The Giver
3. The Achiever
4. The Artist
5. The Observer
6. The Supporter
7. The Optimist
8. The Leader
9. The Mediator

Number types are arranged clockwise around a circle and are clustered into threes and identified as 'gut' (8, 9, 1), 'heart' (2, 3, 4), and 'head' (5, 6, 7), which give further clues as to how a person makes sense of the world around them. For each number type there is a cluster of behaviours or character traits which identify strengths and weaknesses, even predilective sin. It is important to emphasise that although it is understood that an individual's basic personality type does not change, there is a dynamic of transformation to be worked on that brings one through from what the exponents call an 'unredeemed' or 'immature' personality to a 'redeemed' and 'mature' personality, the latter being defined as a reflection of Christlike virtue. The process of 'working on' less strong characteristics is similar to the adoption of 'shadow' characteristics in the MBTI.

With only nine personality types to choose from, there is a danger of stereotyping. It is also important to understand that it is down to the individual to identify themselves from the nine types offered. The subject does not necessarily receive a bespoke suit of clothes but they do know what suits them from the range available 'off the peg'. The interpretation of type is enriched by the concept of 'wings' which allows that personal characteristics can be identified from neighbouring type numbers. For example a Nine may show characteristics from either the neighbouring One or the neighbouring Eight.

The Enneagram is like an onion: there is no centre as such, only layers of understanding. The critical literature refers to international conferences on the Enneagram and to an ongoing discovery of all it has to offer. One wonders if it will be as popular in Europe as it is in the USA and whether it will feature as often as the MBTI does in programmes or events aimed at helping people to a deeper understanding of who they are before God and how they relate to others.

Before leaving this brief description of the Enneagram it is worth noting that the acquisition of self-knowledge is not its only function. It is also meant to draw a person towards God through a transformative process, helping them to find their 'true self' as they enter more deeply into the process. According to Rohr & Ebert the Sufis call the Enneagram 'Full face of God' because they see nine energies manifested in the nine personality types and regard them as attributes of God ('nine reflections of divine light').[55] They argue that the Enneagram is not the answer to the quest for self-knowledge but that it is one signpost among many. Signposts, they assert, show the way, but the individual has to follow the way using the Enneagram as a cognitive model and that 'Christians see in Jesus Christ the face of God: the God become human, the revealer and revelation of divine love.'[56]

---

55. Ibid, p.232.
56. Ibid, p.xiv.

A closer look at Marston's work

The Personal Profile Analysis (PPA) is a psychometric instrument developed and licensed by Thomas International, a worldwide concern that provides people assessments which empower business leaders to transform the performance of their teams and individuals. The PPA differs from both the Enneagram and the MBTI in four important ways:

1. It allows for personality to change over a period of time. Having said that, to what extent the personality can change is not explained in either of Marston's works.

2. Many psychologists would agree that multifaceted psychometric tools, as well as a multiplicity of such tools, are likely to offer a more rounded appraisal of personality type, though they would share the view that psychometric tools have only a supportive role to play in psychological science and psychopathological treatment. We might hold that it is a case of 'the more the merrier'. In this, PPA offers considerably more indices than either MBTI (16 indices) or the Enneagram (nine indices). This allows for some 'fine tuning' in interpretation. As with MBTI and the Enneagram, the interpretation is based on a self-scoring (as with MBTI) and a self-reporting (as with the Enneagram) methodology. Thomas International claim 85 per cent accuracy in results and emphasises (as do the other two tools studied) that PPA is a tool to be used only in conjunction with discussion.

3. Goldsmith and Wharton state that MBTI does not measure (among other things) stress in the individual,[57] whereas PPA does measure work-related stress. It should be noted that when completing the self-report proforma,

---

57. M. Goldsmith & M. Wharton, *Knowing Me, Knowing You*, p.9.

the PPA administrator asks the subject to think of themselves in the work setting. I sense that this is not the case with MBTI.

4. Environment alters behaviour and people react and respond to behavioural environments according to whether they are basically extroverted or introverted. Extroversion/introversion, as a key determinant, resonates with Carl Jung's work on personality type.

In the second half of his book, Marston expounds theories of how people manifest love – both active and passive love behaviour. This might have value to us in relation to how people see themselves before God, especially in response to the Lord's injunction to love God and our neighbour[58] but it would seem that Marston's approach to love is more *erotic* than *agapéic*.

Unlike the other two tools under consideration, PPA does not purport to have a God-centred personal growth orientation. However, the results give clear insight into problems with work–life balance, and scoring frequently leads to discussion about what is important in life and about the difficulties people can have in the workplace when their own moral values are compromised. More than that, PPA is used to help people make appropriate career choices, and in this there is an implicit intention to match life work to gifting and calling; this is interpreted by many subjects as giving clues to how best to serve God and their neighbour.

Three psychological tools compared and contrasted

Goldsmith and Wharton assert that personality type is dynamic and not static, which means that it is a process: it

---

58. Luke 10:27.

is changing and developing all the time.[59] They say that Jung believed that we are born with our own 'ideal type' but that it may take us a long time to discover it. They argue that our background and training, our environment and the pressures that we live under, can all serve to hide or skew our fundamental type. There is a distinction here between the claims of MBTI and those of Marston. The former, according to Goldsmith and Wharton, contend that basic personality type needs to be discovered beneath layers of influence whereas Marston asserts that personality is more fundamentally altered by external and internal influences. The Enneagram stands alone in asserting that personality type is not only fairly crudely defined (having fewer indices by which it is measured than either of the other two), but is also fixed in a person throughout their lifetime.

These differences raise the question of how free we are to migrate from one personality type to another. When we appear to do so we may only be uncovering a deeper knowledge of our true personality type. Alternatively, we may be acting out a personality type in order to get through life successfully. I am reminded of the words of King George III in the film *The Madness of King George*, when he reported to his family that he had forgotten how to 'seem' but that now he had recovered a sense of that, recognising that it was more important for the people that he acted 'seemly' than that he was himself. But how free are we to act out of type? What are the long-term consequences of having to adopt alien character traits? Goldsmith and Wharton argue, 'for Carl Jung the distinction between Extroversion and Introversion is the most important one between people,

---

59. M. Goldsmith & M. Wharton, *Knowing Me, Knowing You*, p.38.

because it describes the source, direction and focus of their energy'. They argue that, 'whether at home, at work, or at school, the extent to which we are able to resort to the preferred source of our energy will have a significant effect upon the quality of our daily lives.'[60] Does this suggest that our behaviour becomes who we are?

On the issue of validation, it seems that the psychological tools studied are validated chiefly by the subject who has provided the responses to the questions put to them. One dimension of the validation of self-scoring/reporting psychological tools is the historicity and commonality of the archetypical and stereotypical constructs people use to describe their own personality and that of others. In the Enneagram there are no questions except that when one is reading the detailed descriptions of the nine personality types one asks oneself, 'Is this me?' Kline records serious doubts about the way personal questionnaires are validated, especially those which purport to measure criteria not based on sound scientific evidence. He concludes that whereas 'extroversion' and 'anxiety' have a psychological basis, indices of 'agreeableness' or 'openness' do not.[61] Thus one may conclude that a psychometric instrument that purports to measure a combination of scientifically measurable results and intuitively assessed factors will reduce or negate an instrument's scientific validity and, thus, its reliability as a tool. On this basis, there is no external scientific and objective methodology of validation in any of the three tools. However, how one understands oneself to be is, arguably, more important than who one is perceived to be by others, and is a sound basis for self-awareness and self-improvement.

---

60. Ibid, p.20.
61. P. Kline (2000), *A Psychometrics Primer*, London: Free Association Books, p.101.

If we accept that self-reporting tools such as these accurately reveal insights into personality characteristics and behaviour, we could expect that the 'results' obtained from each of the three tools would be similar. The value of a multi-dimensional approach (i.e. using more than one tool) would be similar to the value of asking someone the same question three different ways. The interlocutor would be providing an opportunity for fresh expressions that would make for a fuller overall response. They would seem to offer a language for the expression of self-truths: a language in three dialects with which to articulate self-knowledge. The liberative quality of identifying one's own personality and its traits and attributes is that it frees us from an imperative to try to act or behave out of character more often than is necessary to sustain social relations and to achieve personal goals.

These may be blunt instruments but they make a contribution to people's understanding of themselves. Perhaps their greatest value is in the conversation they generate about how we see ourselves and how we relate to others.

Psychological tools and developing spirituality

The value of MBTI to our developing spirituality in a ministry of discernment has been attested to by Gordon Jeff, a leading figure in spiritual direction and in the training of spiritual directors. Jeff writes:

> We have found the MBTI so valuable that we have expected all participants on our courses to have attended a basic course by the beginning of the second year of their spiritual direction course, either a basic course run by ourselves or a good one elsewhere. We insist with our own courses on at least ten hours of working time for a basic course.[62]

---

62. G. Jeff (2007), *Spiritual Direction for Every Christian*, p.65.

He suggests that people who have been on a more perfunctory course have seldom learned enough for them to use the system in their work or relationships. Jeff asserts:

> MBTI has helped countless spiritual directors to realise that, for example, extroverts, who draw energy from the outer world, are likely to be helped to pray in different ways from introverts, who draw energy from their inner world. Or again, 'head' and 'heart' people respond differently to God, but no one is better than any other, just different.[63]

In the latter half of the quotation Jeff is using the language of the Enneagram when he writes of 'head' and 'heart'.

The key to helping people through the use of psychological tools is to help them to discover how to live a fulfilled life in the person they are, the person created by God and called into discipleship. Psychological tools have a place in the vast field of the discernment of vocation and in the ordinariness of a spiritual director–directee relationship, but such tools need to 'know their place' in the wider discernment of what God is bringing to the life of both parties. Much will depend, too, on the skill of the administrator and the willingness of the subject to honestly explore who they are before God and how best they might serve him.

There is, of course, more to our human identity than our personality type. Spirituality, the way we pray and relate to God, is affected also by gender, by sexuality, by our cultural roots or conditioning and by age (chronologically and experientially). This is helpfully explored by Richard Rohr in *Falling Upward: A Spirituality for the Two Halves of Life*.[64]

---

63. Ibid, p.66.
64. R. Rohr (2011), *Falling Upward: A Spirituality for the Two Halves of Life*, San Francisco: Jossey-Bass.

CHAPTER FOUR

Life happens!

Life happens to us all! Life shapes our view of God and colours our view of relationships both celestial and temporal. Continuing the theme of spirituality as contextual to everyday life, we consider how life shapes us. As we listen to the people around us we are likely to hear accounts of things that happened to them and how such events and circumstances, both positive and negative, shaped how they relate to God. We are likely to hear how their theological reflection is based largely on their experience. Where and how God met them in a particular circumstance is balanced with reflection on how God seemed to relate to them: close, maybe, or distant, even absent. They will describe how events made them stronger or nearly destroyed them, or how they battled against cynicism, or how they remain bitter or angry with God, the Church, or life in general. Their stories encourage us to appraise how life has shaped our own spirituality, our theology and our relationships.

Let us reflect on our experience of 'finding', 'losing', 'binding', 'loosing': how we found love, insight, epiphany moments, new confidence, self-worth, self-belief, consolation, acceptance, voice, articulation, forgiveness, absolution, the grace to forgive or to let go. We explore how life may have been shaped by loss: loss of perspective, loss of confidence, self-worth, self-belief, and grief as the pain of loss. We consider in what ways we have been 'bound': trapped in a circumstance, or bound by an addiction or an obsession. Let us reflect on who or what has set us free from burdens of sin, shame, guilt; what has been life enhancing and what has been life draining. Reviewing the past and what has shaped our spirituality to date leads to reflection on what we might yet change about our view of God and our celestial and temporal relationships.

It would be easy to infer from the title of this chapter that when life happens to us it happens adversely or tragically, but life happens to us in so many positive ways too. It happens in major events such as falling in love or the birth of a child. It happens to us in memorable holidays or adventures. It happens to us every day in the tiniest of details as well as in the great life-changing occasions of life. If we have an authentic spirituality we will not have lost sight or ceased to care, however, for those whose lives happen in totally adverse circumstances – those who grasp at survival rather than have life-embracing experiences. We know ourselves to be privileged when we can say of our own life that what has happened, or is happening now, brings more joy than sorrow; that expresses to God more gratitude than heart-rending petition.

When we listen to the stories people tell of past tragedies and adversity of many kinds we sometimes hear, too, how through the grace of God, the unconquerable human spirit and the enablement of other people, adversity and tragedy was lived through to a point where life took on a different hue. Death gave way to life. This is at the heart of the Christian message. However, life after tragedy or adversity is not the same as life before. It cannot be so because life experiences shape who we are. We say that they teach us something about ourselves and our ability to survive and to do better than survive. They may teach us, too, about humankind: about friendship, and about how we benefit from the gifts and skills of others.

Life events, adverse and tragic, or joy-making and uplifting, may also change our perception of God. Stories abound of how people have experienced the darkest times of their life and have railed against a God they have come to view as capricious and vindictive, or at the very least disinterested or powerless to help. Life happens, and when it does it changes our theology. This does not mean to say, though, that it always changes our theology in an unhelpful way. Life events challenge what we believe about God, and that can mean having to radically rethink our preconceived ideas of what God is like.

People who have an explicitly Christian faith before tragedy strikes are not immune to the challenge of working through their understanding of God; indeed, they may be at a disadvantage compared with the nominal believer or agnostic whose expectations of how God will act in a particular circumstance may be much lower. This holds true not only for personal encounters with suffering or tragedy but with situations where we seek to witness or minister to others in times of 'trouble, sorrow, need, sickness or any other adversity'.[65]

As life events change our theology, they also change our spirituality, because our spirituality is relational to God. As our relationship develops so does its articulation in prayer – its deepest meaning in the silence of our hearts.

Miriam's story

Miriam, who came to faith as a teenager, describes how she found great comfort in the company of and in conversation with Jesus, but she could never address God as 'Father' because a driving factor in her seeking and finding consolation

---

65. Communion service, *The Book of Common Prayer*, Cambridge University Press.

in the company of Christians was her need to escape, regularly, from a despotic and overbearing father. Miriam had always found it difficult to pray the Lord's Prayer because she could not get past the opening phrase, 'Our Father . . .'.

Life had happened for Miriam and it had shaped her theology and therefore her spirituality. Many years later, after she had married and become a parent, she saw a different model of 'fathering' in her husband's relationship with their children. The life happenings of marriage and parenthood changed her understanding of the parenting of God. Not only was Miriam able to address God as 'Father' but also she had no problem with those who addressed God as 'Mother'; she let go of an over-specific notion of God in gender terms. This freed her to relate to God in a deep way whilst she lost nothing of her relationship with Jesus and a growing sense of the dynamic of her relationship with God in the gentle nurture of the Holy Spirit.

St Ignatius of Loyola (1491–1556)

The life and spirituality legacy of Ignatius may help us as we consider how life happens and how it changes our view of God, of ourselves and of the world in general. According to one Jesuit-owned website, Ignatian spirituality may be defined as 'a spirituality for everyday life. It insists that God is present in our world and active in our lives. It is a pathway to deeper prayer, good decisions guided by keen discernment, and an active life of service to others'.[66]

This spirituality is contemporary with, and is correlational with, the traditions associated with St Teresa of Avila and St John of the Cross, whose writings have influenced

---

66. www.ignatianspirituality.com/what-is-ignatian-spirituality/ (accessed 18 October 2013).

Christians in every century since that time. Their approach to contemplation is in a class of its own and is well worth exploring.

St Ignatius knew a thing or two about how life events shape one's spirituality. He was a Spanish knight born of a noble family from the Basque. After being seriously wounded in the Battle of Pamplona in 1521, he underwent a spiritual conversion while in recovery. Spiritual reading inspired him to abandon his previous military life and to devote himself to the service of God. Against the backdrop of his legacy we consider how life events affect our spirituality and how we might be assisted in both sustaining and recovering our relationships with God, with others and with creation (our spirituality).

Life happened for Ignatius in the form of privilege and position. In those days there was always a battle to fight, and the ladies of the day were always impressed by the sophisticated, swashbuckling knight who rode off to war with a lady's favour tucked into his belt. Ignatius could have expected to inherit family wealth and lands and to have enjoyed all the good things in life, or to have died heroically in battle. He could have enjoyed all that life had offered him to date (and he probably did), and there is nothing wrong with that! It is so easy to assume that in order to lead a deeply spiritual life we need to give up everything that is good, delicious, exciting, satisfying or adventurous. Jesus tells us that he came that we 'might have life, and have it abundantly'[67] – a subject to which we shall return in Chapter six.

It wasn't, however, in the lifestyle of a Spanish nobleman that Ignatius found his deep and personal relationship with God. The trigger for his conversion was adversity: a

---

67. John 10:10.

wounding serious enough to be life threatening and certainly serious enough to stop him in his tracks, causing him to face up to what his life was about. He stopped long enough to read something inspirational. There are many Christians who can testify to a time, a moment of conversion, when their understanding of what their life is about took on a radically different perspective. This was Ignatius' experience too. From that moment of conversion he went on to become a priest, to found the Society of Jesus (Jesuits), and to leave a legacy of a tradition in spirituality that has enabled countless Christians to live close to the Lord.

Ignatius, through his writing and his wisdom, demonstrates something very important for us in our exploration of how life affects our spirituality. He draws not only from his post-conversion life but also from his life before that. He does not dismiss his pre-conversion lifestyle as entirely contrary to and in conflict with Christian discipleship. Rather, he focuses our attention upon the goodness and generosity of God. He does not suggest that poverty is a good thing for everyone but rather that to enjoy the good things of life is God's desire for all. Ignatius' spirituality is incarnational and real, and in deep joy and gratitude to God he encourages us to seek and find the goodness of God in all God's generous provision.

The spirituality of Ignatius is based in the truth of God revealed in Christ: God's plan of salvation and what St Paul calls the mystery of Christ.[68] According to George Ganss, Ignatius' constant endeavour was to make all his activities result in praise or glory to God.[69] He understood eternal self-fulfilment to be the purpose of life on earth. Although

---

68. Romans 16:25, 26.
69. G. E. Ganss (ed.) (1991), *Ignatius of Loyola: Spiritual Exercises and Selected Works*, New Jersey: Paulist Press.

Ignatius went on to study theology, if there had been such a science in those days, one could have imagined that he had studied positive psychology! Tom Carson, an Anglican priest writing in *The Way*, explores the relationship between Ignatian spirituality and positive psychology which he considers through the lens of 'gratitude'.[70] Being grateful and finding something to be glad about are very close cousins and a powerful antidote to dolefulness and disgruntlement.

In times of adversity, keeping perspective and managing our mood can be quite a challenge. We use 'self-talk' – a kind of bathroom-mirror counselling to try to keep our life in perspective. 'Come on,' we might say to ourselves in the bathroom mirror, 'you've met worst challenges. You're a survivor. You can beat this!' Sometimes it works. Sometimes, however, we need rather more help, perhaps in the form of encouragers, supporters, counsellors or therapists. Those suffering from severe depression or who are in the depths of grief or despair are likely to need a little more than sterling self-effort to engender a positive mental attitude. Severe depression and allied pathology can drain energy away so that personal resources for 'sterling efforts' are not easily come by. Into this, and into other aspects of the human condition, St Ignatius demonstrates amazing insight, and his suggestions for coping with everyday life and for sustaining a deep and fulfilling relationship with God are timeless, invaluable and apposite, and they enjoy universal acclaim.

We all have techniques for cheering ourselves up on a bad day, but 'cheering up' may be a hopelessly superficial and inadequate treatment for a profound depression or despair. Some psychologists, however, suggest that many people suffer, at one time or another, from a low-grade chronic

---

70. *The Way*, 52/2 (April 2013), 7–19.

depression that can be managed by changing our mindset and keeping things in perspective. Mindfulness techniques, once thought to be the sole province of Buddhists, are finding their way into secular and Christian helping, both professional and informal. Conversations with aficionados has revealed to me intriguing connections between Ignatian spirituality and mindfulness techniques. One gift from Ignatian spirituality springs to mind in this respect: the identification of the seemingly polarised concepts of consolation and desolation. Ignatius teaches:

> By consolation I mean that which occurs when some interior motion is caused within the soul through which it comes to be inflamed with love of its creator and Lord. Similarly is this consolation experienced when the soul sheds tears which move it to love for its Lord – whether they are tears of grief for its own sins, or about the Passion of Christ our Lord, or about matters directly ordered to his service and praise. Finally under the word consolation I include every increase in hope, faith and charity (love), and every interior joy which calls and attracts one toward heavenly things and to the salvation of one's soul, by bringing it tranquillity and peace in its Creator and Lord.[71]

By desolation Ignatius means everything which is the contrary of what is described above as consolation: 'darkness of soul, turmoil within, an impulsive motion toward low or earthly things, or disquiet from various agitations and temptations.' He asserts that these 'move one toward lack of faith and leave one without hope and without love. One is completely listless, tepid, and unhappy, and feels separated from our Creator and Lord.' Ignatius instructs that during a time of desolation we should not change a decision or a

---

71. G. E. Ganss, *Ignatius of Loyola: Spiritual Exercises and Selected Works*, p.202.

determined course of action but that 'one should remain firm and constant in the proposals and in a decision one made in a time of consolation'. Here Ignatius refers to the discernment of spirits. He asserts, 'For just as the good spirit is chiefly the one who guides and counsels us in time of consolation, so it is the evil spirit who does this in time of desolation. By following his counsels we can never find the way to a right decision.' He does not suggest that we do nothing in a time of desolation. He advises, for example, that we pray and meditate more, thus leaning towards the 'good spirits'.

Holding on to a consolatory mindset and to 'every interior joy which calls and attracts us toward heavenly things and to the salvation of one's soul' is not always easy, but if we are apt to dwell too much on life's desolations it can be a good way to try to keep some perspective, a balanced view of our life as it is currently experienced. This key injunction is extremely important to maintaining a hopeful and balanced perspective on life. Perhaps the reader might like to consider an important decision that was made during a time of consolation – perhaps the acceptance of a proposal of marriage or the decision to pursue a vocational calling. Do you also recall times when you felt quite desolate about life and were tempted to reverse what had been a good decision in a former more consolatory mood? It can be very helpful to revisit the mood one was in when that major decision was made – when there was joy and optimism and a sense of adventure. Perhaps, in reality, nothing has actually changed; there is nothing to warrant a change of course from the one set at that time. There may be no good reason, in a time of darkness, doubt, fear or distress (desolation) to change that good decision. Ignatius advises waiting until a time of consolation or until one can mentally revisit the last time of consolation in order to examine the continuing validity of a decision once made. Review your decisions, he suggests, but not now!

Like so many practices in our spiritual relationships with God, with other people and with the world in general, the maintenance is more a matter of discipline, of steeling ourselves to keep going. (Remember to 'Wax on, wax off'!) Here Ignatius offers us a practice that can feel a bit like a discipline when we are not of a mind to apply ourselves but which is for many people a life-giving daily exercise. Ignatius calls it 'The Examen'.

The Examen

On the whole, examination of conscience exercises tend to focus on sin, on thoughts, words or deeds that have led us away from God. Examining our consciences and bringing our sins to God for forgiveness is a good thing to do, and to do regularly. The Examen, however, is more than that. The Examen is an appraisal of our relationship with God, once or twice a day. We consider both consolation and desolation experienced since the previous Examen and pray in response to the exercise. Ignatius offers a detailed process for the Examen.

It is helpful to set a pattern for the undertaking, though with practice it may become less consciously and less explicitly structured. It should always begin with reminding ourselves of God's great love for us, which leads to a reflection on the quality of our loving response. Next we consider what has happened in our life since the last Examen, and give thanks for God's goodness. We invoke the Holy Spirit to illumine our hearts and minds so that we can review honestly how we have behaved towards God, to others or to ourselves. Finally, we talk to Jesus, sharing with him our hopes and fears, our aspirations and our good intentions as well as expressing sorrow or regret for our sins.

Tom's experience of the Examen

I asked Tom if he had found Ignatius' Examen helpful. Tom responded,

> The Examen is a really wonderful way of trying to find out how God has been moving in your life. As you review the day with gratitude, you can see moments where God has been close to you, even if you didn't know it at the time. It also helps you work out what hasn't been quite so good and come to terms with that. As you do the Examen more, you begin to think at certain moments throughout the day, 'Hey – I think I'm going to be grateful for this later,' and you gradually find more of where God is in your life.

An example of a balanced appraisal

Let us imagine that during the course of a very trying morning at work there have been constant interruptions, a heated exchange with a colleague, an unsympathetic response to someone's bad news, and a time of tedious routine tasking that has made us tetchy or irritable. There is enough in there to sieve through and find nuggets of sin to bring to God for forgiveness; but where does that leave us as we tuck into our lunchtime sandwich? Does it leave us feeling low about ourselves, despairing that there isn't a charitable bone in our body? Unloved and unlovely? Maybe just a bit flat? Even with the consolation of God's forgiveness we can still be left feeling wretched and open to negative, even malevolent influences: voices that tell us we are rubbish when it comes to Christian virtue.

This exercise will have been an examination of conscience but it will not have been an Ignatian Examen! For that we would have spent just as long reflecting on the *consolations* of the morning: the warm hug from someone at home as we left for work, the cheerfulness of fellow passengers, the greetings of colleagues, the delicious coffee that was so welcome mid-morning, the tasks completed and the compliment received, the progress made. When we balance consolation with desolation we may find our prayers to God over our sandwich are as much about gratitude as about regret, that our mindset is a little less negative and that we are less prey to the voices of the elemental spirits that seek to devalue us in the eyes of God and in our own eyes.

Is it merely playing the 'glad game'?

The reader may be familiar with the story of Pollyanna, the little girl with indomitable optimism who could find, and who taught a whole community to find, something to be glad about. Pollyanna is at one and the same time endearing and very irritating indeed! If we are honest, there are times when we don't want to be made glad. We are quite content to be grumpy and hard done by, yet we are drawn back to the compelling love of God in Christ who woos us through our grumpiness, our gloominess and despondency and, in spite of ourselves, makes us glad – glad to know him, glad to be alive in him.

Let us not confuse 'gladness' with happiness. Happiness is a rather fickle emotion that hovers about on the surface of us, sometimes in sight and sometimes out of sight. But to be made glad is to be filled with joy in the very depths of our being. Joy, as a gift and fruit of the Holy Spirit, is too deeply implanted in us to be destroyed by emotional upheaval or the uncertainties of daily life. To be made glad is to be en-joyed – to enjoy, at a very deep level, the intimacy of our relationship with God and to know ourselves en-joyed by the Living God. Over time, by faithfully responding to the invitation to come, we are made glad. Like the two disciples on the road to Emmaus, comparing notes after breaking bread with the risen Lord, we ask one another the question, 'Were not our hearts burning within us?' which translates just as well as: 'Were we not made glad?'[72]

Ignatian Spiritual Exercises

A more in depth and extensive appraisal of life and Christian discipleship which came from Ignatius' own experience, writing and teaching are the 'Spiritual Exercises'. The Ignatian Spirituality website quoted earlier summarises the exercises as follows:

> The Spiritual Exercises grew out of Ignatius Loyola's personal experience as a man seeking to grow in union with God and to discern God's will. He kept a journal as he gained spiritual insight and deepened his spiritual experience. He added to these notes as he directed other people and discovered what 'worked'.[73]

With the rise in popularity of Ignatian spirituality has come also the practice of keeping a journal, as did Ignatius. It is a useful way to record thoughts, feelings, prayers and events. It can help us keep perspective, to recall what, in recent times, has been consolatory and what has been desolatory. Ignatius gathered his journal writings – his prayers, meditations,

---

72. Luke 24:32.
73. http://www.ignatianspirituality.com/ignatian-prayer/the-spiritual-exercises/what-are-the-spiritual-exercises/ (accessed 18 October 2013).

reflections and directions – into a carefully designed framework of a retreat, which he called the 'Spiritual Exercises'. Ignatius wrote that the Exercises 'have as their purpose the conquest of self and the regulation of one's life in such a way that no decision is made under the influence of any inordinate attachment'.[74] He wanted individuals to undertake these Exercises with the assistance of an experienced spiritual director who would help them shape the retreat and understand what they were experiencing. Spiritual directors have been trained in how to guide others through these Exercises since 1533, and it should be noted that Ignatius' writings on this subject are for the guide rather than the exercitant.

Ignatius organised the Spiritual Exercises into four 'weeks'. These 'weeks' are not chronologically determined but spatially determined, though those undertaking them may find that, in their fullest expression, they tend to take about 30 days, making four or five 'contemplations' (prayer times) a day alone with God in complete solitude. The Exercises are a journey into deeper commitment to Christ. Beginning with reflection on God's unconditional love for us, the exercitant is gently confronted with their own sins and failings and is brought back to the call of Christ to follow him. Through passages from Holy Scripture regarding the early life of Jesus and his ministry, the exercitant reflects on their own Christian discipleship, considers accounts of the Passion, death and rising of Christ, and ends with renewal of commitment to follow Christ and practical resolutions for discipleship. When the Exercises are truncated (say to a five- or eight-day programme), the full extent of the journey is

---

74. Paraphrased from the Introduction to the Spiritual Exercises heading [21] (public domain). The text can be found in G. E. Ganss, *Ignatius of Loyola*, p.129.

vital even if there is less time for prayer and contemplation on particular stages in the process.

No substitute for the real thing, but of enormous practical help, are the many contemporary publications based on the Exercises, but it is worth reading them in the original form to get the essence of them. *The Ignatian Workout* by Tim Muldoon is both comprehensible and faithful to the spirit of them. The Exercises are for those who sincerely seek to please and serve God.

Tom's experience of the Spiritual Exercises

Having a young family and full-time employment meant that I wasn't able to make a full 30-day retreat to complete the exercises. So I decided that, for a period of time, I would meet more regularly with my spiritual director and used a book[75] which guided me through the four 'weeks' over a couple of months. I suppose I didn't have the experience that going away to do the exercises would give, but going through the different 'weeks' was profound. The experience opened my eyes in new ways to some of the key aspects of the Christian faith: God's overwhelming love as Creator, the depth and extent of my sins, Christ's love and humility, the difficulty of handing over my debit card to God, finding profound gratitude to God for all things. Most of all, completing the exercises has started me on a journey of trying to find out where God is in all of my life.

When darkness is more than adversity or mood

St John of the Cross (1542–1591), Spanish mystic and reformer of the Carmelite Order, wrote *The Dark Night of the Soul.* In it he describes the darkness and dryness we can

---

75. T. P. Muldoon, (2004), *The Ignatian Workout*, Chicago: Jesuit Way (Loyola Press).

experience in our relationship with God or in our prayerful expression of that relationship. Such has been the influence and abiding legacy of this work that 'dark night' experience has become shorthand in the field of spirituality. 'Dark night' is not so much a mood or a negative attitude towards God, or even a supposed distancing of God from the human soul. It is more a nothingness, a dryness that prevails in spite of our efforts to overcome it. God seems absent. This is closely related to, though different from, a theological and spiritual view that one should not expect anything in the way of an affective experience of God, for God will not be known. Such 'apophatic' prayer in that theological premise expects nothing. Close but different, then, is the experience of 'night' where there is longed-for enlightenment. Horatius Bonar wrote, in a hymn:

> I heard the voice of Jesus say,
> 'I am this dark world's light;
> look unto me,
> thy morn shall rise,
> and all thy day be bright.'[76]

In times of darkness, when the 'morn' of our existence feels anything but bright, it can be a matter of blind obedience to believe that the morn shall rise and all our day be bright: to hold, in faith and obedience, that where Christ is, there is light; that Christ will dispel the pseudo-reality of darkness, and break through in streams of resurrection light. We are not called to be in denial about the darkness we experience, or the darkness experienced by others. Rather we should acknowledge the darkness of the day, the experience, the situation, the circumstance, and own that Christ, the light of

---

76. Horatius Bonar, 1846. Public domain.

the world, is no less present, no less to be found in the dark places of our life or of the lives of those around us. Jesus says, 'I am the light of the world',[77] and he will burst through the darkest places with resurrection light!

In Holy Scripture, 'night' is used metaphorically. People experiencing the 'night' of unbelief or ignorance need the gentle touch. For them, Paul is right. This *is* the hour of crisis, but far from waking out of their sleep,[78] they want desperately to put their head under the bed covers and sink into oblivion. How often, if you are honest, have you encountered times of ignorance or unbelief before the gentle and encouraging light of Christ brings a little glow of new faith, new hope, a rekindling of love for God, for humankind, and for yourself? Christ the light of the world meets us in our ignorance and our unbelief.

Sometimes the spirituality of the dark night comes in the form of adversity and affliction. Surely we can all relate to that! In the metaphysical sense of the word night, adversity and affliction take on a whole new meaning. Pain can seem worse, noises are exaggerated, images are distorted, sensitivities are heightened.

Sometimes, however, night-time is a time to think things through. It is sometimes the only time to think. It is a time to reassess one's situation, to review priorities, to make plans. It can also be the time when things look particularly bleak. Problems seem insurmountable and morale may be at its lowest. Hope gives way to despair. When night-time thinking pervades the daylight hours, life can seem very dire indeed. Again, Christ the light of the world meets us in the hope and healing brought by medical professionals, informal

---

77. John 8:12.
78. Romans 13:11.

carers, relatives, friends, pastors, counsellors, supporters. Slowly, or suddenly, the dawn from on high breaks upon us in restored vision, possible solutions, options and choices.

Night-time in Holy Scripture can also be a metaphor for death, with the trail of grief it leaves behind. It is like the night-time spirituality of the two disciples on the road to Emmaus, sharing their grief and pain at the death of their beloved master. Yet Christ the light of the world meets them on the road and opens to them all that his resurrection means for them and for all humankind. So gladdened are they by the presence of the risen Christ that they turn and walk back to Jerusalem to tell others who are still in the night-time of their grief.[79]

The 'night-time' experienced by those first disciples did gave way to enlightenment; not immediately, not during the horror of the coming days or during the bewilderment of that first Easter Day, but later, after the Spirit came. It happened as they slowly began to understand the significance of the Passion, death and rising of Jesus, and the realisation of his powerful presence in both times of darkness and times of light. They experience, as do we, that desolation gives way to consolation.

St John the Evangelist carefully comments that the Lord rose whilst it was yet dark.[80] John wants to teach us something about the power of the resurrection of the Lord overcoming the darkness of the night: that the risen Christ is the light of the world. As Bonar puts it in the final verse of his hymn: 'I heard the voice of Jesus say, "I am this dark world's light . . ."'

---

79. Luke 24:13-35.
80. John 20:1.

For John, Jesus is the one who dispels the darkness of the world. Jesus is the light of the world: a light no darkness can overcome. Suddenly we are back to the prologue of St John's Gospel: 'The light shines in the darkness, and the darkness did not overcome it.'[81] We tend to associate the prologue of St John's Gospel with Christmas services, but the point about light in darkness is made just as well at any time of the year. John offers parentheses around the whole Christ event by making the connection between how God entered into human life in the darkness of the world and how he consummates his mission of bringing light to the world by rising from the dead whilst it was yet dark.

It can be difficult to hold on in faith during a 'dark night' experience. The promise of Jesus that he is the light of the world can seem hollow, unreal, incredible. I am reminded of Shakespeare's somewhat 'politically incorrect' play *The Taming of the Shrew*, in which the character Petruchio comes to 'wive it well in Padua' and in haste weds Katherine, the wild and fiercely independent elder daughter of Baptista. Petruchio seeks blind obedience from Katherine and, to test her, he points to the midday sun and proclaims: 'Good Lord, how bright and goodly shines the moon!'

To this Katherine replies: 'The moon? 'Tis the sun.'

Petruchio presses the point: 'I say 'tis the moon that shines so bright', but Katherine insists it is the sun. Finally she must comply, and on they go.

In some ways the risen Lord challenges us to be blindly obedient to his word: that he is this world's true light even when we can see only darkness. In Bonar's words, the risen Lord says, 'Look unto me, thy morn *shall* rise, and all thy day be bright.' When the dawn does break on our

---

81. John 1:5.

understanding, adversity gives way to healing and peace. New life breaks though our many little deaths, enabling us to cry with more enthusiasm, 'Christ is risen! Alleluia!' We can, with deeper joy and conviction, sing the final words of Bonar's hymn:

> I looked to Jesus, and I found
> in him my star, my sun:
> and in that light of life I'll walk
> till travelling days are done.

By our baptism into the death and rising of Christ we carry the light of Christ within us; we take that light into the night-time places of disbelief and ignorance, the night-time lives of suffering and affliction, and the dark night places of spiritual and physical death. But this light we carry is made the brighter because we do not carry it alone: we walk in the light of Christ and we walk together. Together we are the resurrection body of Christ, bringing his light to the night-time places of this world.

In the next chapter we will consider travelling together in God and how God shapes our spirituality.

CHAPTER FIVE

God shaping spirituality in power, presence and participation in the Divine Life

In previous chapters we considered how spirituality is shaped by personality, by life events and by human environmental context. In this chapter we consider how spirituality is shaped by the power and presence of God, through the environment of the Triune God and through participation in the Divine Life. This chapter is about God's nurture of us and about the influence of the Holy Spirit on who we are becoming. It is about being shaped by the grace of God and our transformation into Christlikeness. We reflect on how it is possible, through a process of redaction, for the mystic within us to be revealed in transforming grace through the power, potency and gentleness of the Holy Spirit.

Spirit shaping life

When we reflect on our life, our circumstances or the state of our prayer we can easily suppose that living a fuller, more holy life and enjoying a closer relationship with God is all about *our* initiatives, *our* efforts, but the reality is that our relationship with God, like any other relationship, is a two-way thing. This is the God who has called us into life and into new life in Christ through our baptism into the death and resurrection of Jesus. We are God's creatures and, by God's grace and power, we are a new creation and we grow in holiness chiefly by God's grace at work in us. The death and rising of Jesus is central to our faith. Somehow, through Christ's death and rising, our relationship with God is restored, made sublime, ratified as eternal and drenched in love.

Christians wrestle with differing theologies of how, through the death and rising of Jesus, our relationship with God is made whole. We call them theories of atonement, or 'at-one-ment'. We may have come to the conclusion that there is no entirely satisfactory human understanding or articulation of it, yet we remain no less convicted that the death and rising of Christ has life-changing, world-changing, cosmos-changing significance. We glory in a God who so loved the world that he gave his only Son in order that the world might live.[82]

Over and against that, alongside it, is the conviction that the death and rising of Christ has deep and personal meaning. However we theologise about it there is, at the heart of it, something life-changing about the death and rising of Christ for *me*, and for *you*: my and your eternal destiny is changed. Central to our conviction is the knowledge of God's love for each and every one of us. We glory in a God who loves us all more than we can imagine. What, then, is our response to the God who demonstrates, in the death and rising of Christ, deep and abiding love for the world? Motivated by love and gratitude we want to rush out and tell the good news of God's saving love. We want to engage with the world and its needs. Our response to the actions of God in Christ our Saviour is to take action, to do something to help build God's kingdom of love here on earth. That is all well and good and a subject we will consider in more detail in the next chapter, but sometimes, in our feverish endeavours on God's behalf, we easily overlook one central truth: that

82. John 3:16.

our relationship with God, and all it inspires us to do on God's behalf, is initiated and sustained by God's initiative and sustenance.

As we discovered in an earlier chapter, knowing ourselves is helpful in understanding how best we might worship God, how we might draw closer to God in personal prayer and how we might live a grace-filled life. Knowing ourselves is one thing; knowing God is quite another! God does not intend to be known as such. Having said that, Jesus came to tell us something vitally important about God. Through Jesus, God's nature is revealed. Through the teaching of Jesus we have learned how to relate to God in more intimate terms. Jesus tells us to call God 'Abba' – 'Daddy'[83] – signalling that God wants an intimate relationship with us and with all creation.

Jesus reminds us, 'You did not choose me but I chose you'.[84] We are chosen of the Beloved since the beginning of time. Our home is at the heart of God. It is our default position. So much of our life energy goes into pulling away from our default position as if we are attached to God by a very long elastic band: all the strength goes into pulling away. Often, we will tell ourselves that the energy of pulling is in order to go out and 'do' in the name of God, as if we leave behind the 'being' of our life. One hears the warning: 'Remember we are human beings and not human doings!'

The second half of the verse quoted above would seem to give that 'going out' some authority: 'And I appointed you to go and bear fruit', but nowhere does the Scripture suggest that we 'go out' in our own strength alone or that we should be any less bound up in the presence of God.

---

83. Mark 14:36.
84. John 15:16.

Three major traditions

Introduction

Activity for God is a matter of listening in obedience to what God wants of us. Being with God is a matter of listening to the voice of God calling us into deeper communion; it is a drawing-in into the very heart of God. This understanding of being and doing, of going out yet remaining close to God, brings us to reflect on another major spirituality tradition within the Christian heritage: the Contemplative tradition. Alongside that is the awareness of the powerful presence of God at work in and through us, reminding us that the source of all our energy in the service of God comes from the Holy Spirit. This is the essence of the Charismatic tradition. The proximity to us of God, and of the whole company of heaven, as we go about our work of love in mission and ministry is the spirituality tradition of the great Eastern Orthodox Churches.

It would seem, on the surface of it, that these three traditions have little in common. Indeed, I have seen Christians in a church congregation practically at war with one another as liturgy that is designed to bring a little heaven to earth (as does Orthodox liturgy) is seen as alien to worship that is designed to own the powerful presence of the Holy Spirit. Since a new wave of the Holy Spirit right across the universal Church in the 1970s there has been scepticism, cynicism and alienation within Church congregations on the matter of the charisms of the Holy Spirit, especially prophecy, healing and tongues. If we believe that we have to make an exclusive choice between one tradition and another we can deny ourselves the opportunity of spiritual growth. There is so much God-given richness in all traditions – a point well made by Richard Foster[85] and other writers. Personally, I have no problem swinging a censor full of incense and praying in tongues at the same time!

To aid our reflection on the richness and diversity within the worldwide Church, I offer a 'thumbnail' sketch of the three aforementioned traditions, making comparisons here and there and offering prayer practices and aids to prayer that have come down to us from each. I recognise, however, that these notes will be hopelessly inadequate to do justice to such great traditions in our Christian heritage.

The Contemplative tradition

In Chapter one we recalled St Augustine's prayer: 'You have made us for yourself, Lord, and our hearts are restless until they rest in you.' If we can identify at all with this heartfelt restlessness we have discovered the mystic within us, or at least the hunger to find the mystic within us. We begin to taste heaven where our habitation will be in being with God, taking us from being moralist to mystic. Contemplative prayer is placing at God's disposal our deepest yearning for union with God in Christ. We are drawn into the mystery of God because we stop resisting that draw. Foster calls this tradition 'a life of loving attention to God' and explains:

> We all hunger for a prayer-filled life, for a richer, fuller practice of the presence of God. It is the Contemplative Stream of Christian life and faith that can show us the way into such intimacy with God. This reality addresses the human longing for the practice of the presence of God.[86]

85. R. J. Foster (1998), *Streams of living water: Essential Practices from the Six Great Traditions of Christian Faith*. New York: HarperCollins.
86. Ibid, p.25.

Contemplative prayer is love expressed. It is loving God for God's own sake.

A glance through (or a struggle through!) the writings of St Teresa of Avila (1515–1582), especially *The Interior Castle*, or those of St John of the Cross (1542–1591) can make union with God in prayer seem out of the reach of us mere mortals, but we have to remember that the imagery and the language of sixteenth-century Spain is quite different from that of the modern idiom. Monastic isolation, regular fasting and penance is the province of comparatively few, but being drawn into God for the love of God and for God's own sake, gazing lovingly on God and allowing God to gaze lovingly on us is not just for the fanciful few. Being still and silent long enough and adopting a disposition of openness does bring its challenges. It is about letting go of certain expectations and holding on in openness to the unexpected. From some who have tried this approach to prayer, we may hear, 'I tried it but it didn't do a thing for me!' Adoration of the God who loves us to bits is not meant to do anything for us! However, once we let go of the expectation that it should, and hold that it might, it sometimes does!

A time of conscious prayer is a process. By that I mean we enter a time of prayer in a particular mood or a sense of where we are before God. For those who seek a 'purpose' in prayer, other than that of attending on God, and who seek some kind of demonstrable outcome, it might be helpful to begin a time of attending on God by noting what mood we are in. At the end of the prayer time we could then note whether anything has changed. When we spend time with God the Beloved we should expect to be affected by it, changed by it even by the slightest degree. For example, did we begin the time of prayer feeling angry with someone, having had a row with them? Did we end the prayer with a sense of being chastened by God, forgiven, calmer now and with the grace to go and try to make up with the person with whom we had the row? We had not focused on the feeling or the row; we focused on God for God's own sake, but our encounter changed us!

Other objections we hear are centred around time and space. We may say we don't have time to take ourselves apart from the demands of everyday life. Contemplative prayer, the contemplation of the presence of God, is not confined to mountainside isolation. There is a need to cultivate a sense of the presence of God in our everyday life, with the God with whom we can commune in the micro gaps between a myriad of daily tasks. Remember that union with God is our default position. Microseconds of attending on God for God's own sake are glimpses of our true habitat.

Exterior and interior silence

Attending on God – seeking the face of God with our inside 'eyes' and listening to God with our inside 'ears' – is made easier by the avoidance of distractions, which usually come in the form of conversation or other external stimuli. Some people find it difficult to cope without conversation or external stimuli whilst others long for time without these distractions but find little opportunity for it in their daily life. This causes us to seek it where we can find it, perhaps by making a retreat (see Chapter seven). The reality for most of us is that protracted periods of silence are hard to come by (indeed, total silence as the absence of all sound is almost impossible!).

A habitat where there is the absence of speech and a *comparatively* quiet environment occasions an opportunity for attending on God without speaking. We call this 'exterior silence', but this is only part of the experience of Christians throughout our history. With practice and patience we can learn to attend on God in the silence of our heart, whether the environment is conducive or not. We can come to know a still and silent place of attending on God to which we can relocate in the microseconds between engagement with the world around us. Then a time of prayer becomes a time of conscious and unconscious attending, an engagement with God by God's own invitation. The cultivation of this kind of attending on God we call 'interior silence'.

Difficulties with prayer

If we are in a right relationship with God, and if we are not overwhelmed by a life crisis, we may still have a hard time praying, perhaps for more mundane reasons. It would be a pity if precious time with God were to be undermined or marred by a problem that could be avoided. We may be too cold or too hot to pray. It may be too early in the morning or too late at night. We may be able to cope with a time of prayer if only we could cope with distractions.

Nowhere is going to be without sound. We could find a deserted beach on which to pray but there would be the sound of the sea withdrawing over a pebble beach, and the sound of seagulls overhead. Such sounds, when joyfully accepted, can enhance our prayer experience. Sudden noises are a different matter, but so many sounds and noises are simply nature, creation, the world getting on with its normal business. We can learn to 'sit light' to them, to accept that they are doing their own God-given thing!

Other distractions come from within us and can be harder to deal with. People, places, circumstances and matters of concern crowd our thoughts. With practice we may find we can behold such thoughts as the mind doing its thing. We need not attend on them too much. They will all still be there at the end of our prayer time. We can keep our inside eyes and ears fixed on God whilst the 'white noise' of our thoughts babbles like a brook around us. This is better than steeling ourselves to put up with the distraction. We may feel a smug glow of martyrdom as we put up with distractions; we turn it into a virtue, like wearing a 'hair shirt', but the attention we give such vainglorious thoughts is attention away from the beloved who has called us into this special place of deep encounter. Praying to God through gritted teeth is hardly ever helpful. It is not the same as bringing our anger and frustration honestly to God. That we should do! We need to draw a distinction between minor irritants that are distracting us in prayer and major rages that ought to be brought to God for resolution.

It may be, however, that the cause of a distraction in prayer is meant to be the focus of it. Without taking our eyes and ears off God we can allow a person, a cause or a concern to be brought into the space. We need not form words to tell God about it – or worse, to tell God what to do about it. We simply hold the situation in the presence of God. Once the situation is acknowledged before God, it may rest there awhile. It is rather like a cat that purrs and seeks attention. Give it a stroke and it may just settle on your lap, allowing your focus of attention to be elsewhere. I have written on this subject before, recognising that we may all, from time to time, have a *Hard Time Praying?* [87] Sometimes, however, the best way to deal with distractions is the removal of them. If you are hungry, go and eat! If you need to make a phone call, make it!

---

87. R. Tomkinson (2009), *Hard Time Praying?*, Buxhall: Kevin Mayhew Ltd.

Spending time with God is not simply a matter of making space for it in the diary. We need a certain resolve to turn up even if we don't really feel like it. If we are regularly too tired for our planned appointments with God, it may be that we are choosing the wrong time of the day. Turning up or 'tuning in' wherever we are is not just for when we feel strong and energetic. Sometimes such occasions find us treating prayer time like a visit to the gym: we are full of muscular prayer and end up breathless for all that we have put in to it. Yet God comes to us not only when we are strong and able to put in boundless energy to make the relationship work. God comes when we have nothing to offer; when we are weary and drained of resources. For those who are ill, anxious or weary, prayer time may be characterised by chronic fatigue, pain, anxiety, worry or fear. Such factors cannot be dismissed as mere distractions from true prayer. They *are* the prayer. Jesus said of his disciples, 'If these were silent, the stones would shout out.'[88] Read that as, 'Even if I were to keep silent, my aching bones or my aching heart would cry out for me.' To those who are wearied by pain, anxiety, fatigue or whatever, many methods of prayer may be less than helpful. To them I commend what I call 'the prayer of the lap of the Lord'.

As you lie down to go to sleep you may have brought to bed with you your worries, your pain, your despair; the guilt of things left undone or handled badly. As you lay your head on your pillow, imagine that you are kneeling at the foot of the Lord who is seated by you. Imagine your head resting on his lap. Smell the linen of your pillow and smell the Lord's garment. You have come to touch the hem of that garment, to find his strength, his healing, his forgiveness and his

88. Luke 19:40.

peace. Bring to him all that weighs you down and feel the weight of your head on his lap. Don't fear that your weight is too much for him to bear. Remember he took the weight of the sins of the world upon him. Rest now, and ask him for the gift of sleep. You have not stopped praying. Hopefully you will doze or sleep. You may not wake refreshed but you need not add to your troubles the anxiety that you have not prayed. Let the wonder of a 24-hour relationship with God change your understanding of both prayer and of rest.[89]

In these circumstances, we come to realise that prayer is no effort of ours at all. It is the Spirit of God at work in us, in wakefulness and vigilance, and in rest and sleep:

> Likewise the Spirit helps us in our weakness; for we do not know how to pray as we ought, but that very Spirit intercedes for us with sighs too deep for words. And God, who searches the heart, knows what is in the mind of the Spirit, because the Spirit intercedes for the saints according to the will of God.[90]

Waking or sleeping, we become increasingly conscious of the God of Activity and the God of Repose. We develop another sense that utilises all our senses. Perhaps we call it numinous. What I mean by that is a sense of the awe and wonder of God, of his enveloping presence, of his power.

Sometimes life events or circumstances have a similar effect on us. At times of great stress or anxiety our senses can be heightened. We can be hypersensitive to a clumsy word from a friend, or easily moved to tears in the most unlikely of situations or circumstances. Out of the darkness and the pain can come incredible emotional and spiritual growth. It

---

89. First published in R. Tomkinson (2000), *Come to Me: A Resource for Weary Christians and Those Who Care About Them*, Kevin Mayhew Ltd.
90. Romans 8:26, 27.

may be some time after the event that we realise that the hand of God was upon us. We begin to see the possibility of the text from the Book of Revelation: 'See, I am making all things new.'[91] This time of heightened sensual awareness is also a time when we can discover the presence of God. New senses are awakened, perspectives are changed, perceptions are altered. In this way we have not only allowed the distraction but we have let it become our prayer.

We may say we have little or no opportunity for a time of prayer. People are worried and distracted by so many things like Jesus' friend Martha,[92] and to be like her sister Mary and sit at the feet of Jesus is a luxury we cannot afford. In reality, we have to be both. Our human relationships exist whether we are directly in touch with one another or not. It is the same with God. In history, spiritual writers have always advocated that we cultivate a sense of the presence of God wherever we are and whatever we are doing, and that we are aware that we can pray anywhere and at any time.

Contemplative spirituality, then, is not just for cloistered religious. It is not beyond our reach but is simply resting in the presence of God: being in a lover's tryst with God, open to all that God might wish to bring yet expecting nothing more than the consolation of God's love. It is an encounter with the Holy God in the ordinariness of our lives. Holiness in ordinariness is at the heart of the Contemplative tradition, and it is also at the heart of the Orthodox tradition.

The Orthodox tradition

Orthodox spirituality is a generic term for the spirituality traditions emerging from the Churches of the East – traditions

---

91. Revelation 21:5.
92. Luke 10:40-2.

seeped in history and rich in treasures too voluminous to cover adequately in this book. In this smorgasbord of spirituality tradition they are the wondrous and exotic tastes of heaven on earth. We can but explore broad principles and practices which will give us a flavour of Orthodox spirituality and invite us to explore further.

Symeon Lash opens his discourse on the subject by asserting that the

> essentials of Orthodox spirituality are summed up in the words which introduce the Lord's Prayer at the Divine Liturgy: 'And count us worthy, Master, with boldness and uncondemned to dare call upon you, the heavenly God, as Father and to say: Our Father . . .'[93]

The Lord's Prayer, the gift of Jesus to us to call upon the Father and inspired to pray in us by the Holy Spirit, thereby invokes the Holy Trinity. Through prayer, we mere human beings, with all our faults and failings, draw near the divine and triune God. We are drawn into the community of the Holy Trinity. At the same time, the divine and utterly holy God deigns to come down among us, to become one of us in the incarnation of God in Jesus Christ. The Holy Trinity is central to Orthodox spirituality. It is the meeting place of the ordinary with the extraordinary, the fallen with the holy, God and humankind. The emphasis in Orthodox spirituality is on the Divine Presence: the invocation of the holy into the ordinary. The incarnated God is utterly transcendent, absolutely holy and 'dwells in unapproachable light,'[94] and yet he calls humans to be one with him, to become 'participants in the divine nature.'[95] So Orthodox spirituality

---

93. S. Lash, 'Orthodox Spirituality' in G. S. Wakefield (ed.) (1983), *A Dictionary of Christian Spirituality*, London: SCM, p.283.
94. 1 Timothy 6:16.
95. 2 Peter 1:4.

is Trinitarian yet Christocentric: utterly otherworldly yet deeply incarnational. Key words here include 'transcendence', 'immanence' and 'presence'.

Another strong theme in Orthodox spirituality is the importance of Holy Scripture for making God present to us, especially the Holy Gospels which make Christ, the Word made flesh,[96] present to us. The radical separation between God and humankind has been abolished by the Incarnate Word. As St Irenaeus states, 'If the word has been made man, it is so that men may be made gods.'[97] We may, therefore, approach the infinite majesty of God with boldness and confidence.

Orthodox spirituality, incarnational as well as transcendental, brings a fusion of powerful presence and brings not a mixture but an emulsion: the divine, the human and all creation are distinct but shaken and held together by the power of the Holy Spirit. Heaven meets earth through the same Spirit. The poem of the metaphysical poet, Richard Crashaw, summarises this phenomenon beautifully:

Welcome all wonders in one sight!
Eternity shut in a span;
summer in winter; day in night;
heaven in earth, and God in man.
Great little one, whose all-embracing birth,
lifts earth to heav'n, stoops heav'n to earth.[98]

In Orthodox liturgy heaven meets earth – for example, in the invocation of the Holy Spirit over the elements of bread and wine, the 'epiclesis'. We see parallels in Western Eucharistic liturgies where the gesture of the lowering of joined hands

---

96. John 1:1-14.
97. Early Church Father, Bishop and martyr, died c.AD 202. *Against Heresies* Book 5, preface. Public domain.
98. R. Crashaw (c.1613–1649), from the poem 'In the Holy Nativity of our Lord'. Public domain.

over the elements of bread and wine evokes a sense of a fluttering dove – one of the traditional symbols for the Holy Spirit. In the Anglican tradition this gesture accompanies these words:

> Lord, you are holy indeed, the source of all holiness: grant that by the power of your Holy Spirit, and according to your holy will these gifts of bread and wine may be to us the body and blood of our Lord Jesus Christ.[99]

In other rites and liturgies we see hands descend in invocation of the Holy Spirit and in expectation that the divine grace will descend upon needy humankind. Orthodox spirituality is characterised by the sense of a God who is so far above us that God's own self cannot be known, and yet is so deep inside us that we cannot but own the Divine Presence. Awe, wonder, numinous and presence are all part of the Orthodox legacy but not exclusive to it. Does not some of this brief explanation resonate with our own deepest aspiration or experience?

What can we sample from the Orthodox spirituality legacy? There are at least five aspects of Orthodox spirituality tradition that bear reflection. They are: 'The *Philokalia*, the Jesus Prayer, the Communion of saints, the Virgin Mary (*Theotokos*) and the Iconographical tradition. What follows is a thumbnail sketch of each: further tasty morsels from the smorgasbord of Christian spirituality which I hope will tempt the appetite or freshen the palate.

The *Philokalia*

There is a vast body of texts written between the fourth and fifteenth centuries that are known as the *Philokalia*.[100] These

---

99. Holy Communion Service, Eucharistic Prayer 'B', *Common Worship*.
100. φιλοκαλία, 'love of the beautiful'.

writings are accounts of the deepest reflections, insights and spiritual experiences of holy women and men throughout the centuries. They are rich in wisdom. Even if we don't see ourselves as mystics (and we shouldn't rule this out!), by reading the writings of the holy ones of God we can draw close to their mystical encounters. We may even be surprised to discover resonances from our own encounters with the Divine Life.

The Jesus Prayer

The text of the Jesus Prayer runs as follows: 'Lord Jesus Christ, Son of God, have mercy on me, the sinner'.[101]

This prayer has been important to Orthodox spiritual practice since the fourteenth century. It is repeated over and over so that it moves from its initial value as a prayer of acclamation of faith in Jesus Christ as Son of God, through the penitential response to the holiness of God, to a confidence in the mercy of God. With practice, the prayer becomes a mantra which does what all mantra are designed to do – to move us from vocal through mental prayer to prayer of the heart, inculcated deep in the will. It can also be used aspirationally, in time with the breathing, and has the effect of calming us in the presence of God.

The reader might find that, in the repetition of it, the prayer becomes shorter and shorter, leaving one with only the name of Jesus as we inhale and exhale. Devotees of the Jesus Prayer might use no other means of deepening their awareness of the presence of God and in the deepening of their relationship with God. Writers in spirituality sometimes refer to occasions of drawing very close to God as 'thin places'. The prayerful repetition of the Jesus Prayer can

---

101. Κύριε ησο Χριστέ, Υ το Θεο, λέησόν με τ ν μαρτωλόν

engender a very thin place – a close encounter with the Divine Life. For a valuable explanation of the use of the Jesus Prayer, which is becoming increasingly popular in Western Christian spiritual practice, I would recommend a splendid book by Brother Ramon and Simon-Barrington Ward.[102]

This would seem to be the place to recommend the use of mantra in prayer. Mantra can help us into reflection and allow our spirit to soar whilst our lips are occupied with an undemanding and repetitive phrase. This is not unlike the use of the rosary, which some regard as the Western Church's equivalent to the Jesus Prayer of the East. Phrases from Holy Scripture or words of a hymn can be very helpful mantra. In Chapter six we will consider briefly the international contribution to Christian spirituality and life made by the Taizé tradition. Suffice it to mention here that Taizé has given us a whole raft of spiritual songs, many based on Holy Scripture, which are, in fact, sung mantra. When sung with others and allowing free harmonisation, they can be a powerful way into deep communion with God. Sung thus they also highlight the value of the communal journey into God: something which is central to Orthodox spirituality. This brings us to another key dimension of it.

The Communion of saints

The phrase 'the Communion of saints' may be familiar to us from the recitation of the Apostles' creed, but have we ever stopped to ponder on its significance? Let us add to that one other phrase, familiar to those for whom the Eucharist is important to their spiritual life. It is the preface to the Sanctus at the heart of the Eucharistic Prayer. In most

---

102. Brother Ramon and S. Barrington-Ward (2001), *Praying the Jesus Prayer Together*, Oxford: BRF.

traditions it runs something like this: 'Therefore with angels and archangels and with all the company of heaven, we proclaim your great and glorious name . . .'

Here we remind ourselves that we journey into God, not only in the company of our church congregation, whether that be 'where two or three are gathered' in the name of the Lord[103] or a vast throng filling a football stadium, but also with all those who comprise the heavenly host: among them those who have gone before us in faith or in sincere searching for God. As the writer of the letter to the Hebrews puts it, 'since we are surrounded by so great a cloud of witnesses'.[104]

Perhaps we only recall the company of heaven on festivals such as All Saints' Day. However, it is important to remember that every time we celebrate the Eucharist we recall that we, too, belong in the dust cloud of mystery and glory with the countless throng of God's holy ones: with angels and archangels and with all the company of heaven praising God and singing holy songs before a Holy God, who is holy and mighty, holy and immortal, holy and merciful. Early Christians understood the need to recall their fellowship with those who had gone before them: those who had suffered for their faith and who now enjoyed the peace and bliss of heaven. Recognising that they belonged together, they gathered to share their confusion, to share their grief, to retell tales of glory and to allow themselves to be caught up in the mystery of belonging still in the glory of the cosmic Christ.

There has always been a need to know ourselves as belonging within the 'cloud of witnesses'.[105] We are called to

---

103. Matthew 18:20.
104. Hebrews 12:1.
105. Hebrews 12:1.

celebrate faithfulness of the Holy Ones of God, but it is also a celebration of our belonging among them, being caught up in the mystery of the cosmic Christ. Liturgical expression of Orthodox spirituality makes present the thrice-Holy God and the company of the saints; heaven in earth and humankind in heaven.

In Chapter four we considered how life events can affect our spirituality. Some of our life events blind us temporarily. They obscure our vision of God and render us confused or disoriented. Reflecting on cloud as framing our experience of confusion, grief, new-unknowing, mystery and glory puts me in mind of a comment made by Stephen Croft who understands the etymology of the word 'deacon' as 'one who comes through the dust'.[106] This is a reference to the lowliest of servants; the one who takes off the dusty sandals from the tired feet of others; the one on the ground, sitting at the threshold; the one who dwells within the cloud of dust created by the prevailing wind.

We are all 'deacons'. We are coming through the blinding and confusing dust of discipleship and servanthood. We may be feeling our way through a very thick, disabling and disorienting dust cloud, unable to see too far ahead and quickly losing sight of whence we came! Being in the cloud is not all bad news, however. Dust in our eyes and our ears makes us more dependent on one another. It also helps prevent us from making rash judgements about who belongs in the cloud and who does not – something Christians spend a lot of time and energy doing! Mercifully, the dust in our own eyes will also help prevent us from seeing who is in there and who is not – until it is too late for us to judge, as the

---

106. S. Croft (1999), *Ministry in Three Dimensions: Ordination and Leadership in the Local Church*, London: DLT.

cloud of unknowing becomes the cloud of glorious knowing in Christ our King.

This is where we are. This is where we abide: in the dust of everyday servanthood, but also within the cloud of dust of witnesses – both those on earth and those in heaven, recognising the need to trust God and to cling to one another in our confusion and grief as we wait for the dust to give way to glory. Engaged in everyday servanthood we can easily forget that we dwell in the dust cloud of the faithful ones of God, both here and in heaven.

The Virgin Mary (*Theotokos*)

Although we reflected briefly on Mary in Chapter one, here we consider her in more depth and through the lens of the Orthodox tradition, which has always held her as exemplary among the Holy Ones of God. It is a mistake to believe that Mary is considered on a par with God. It is a mistake made by people, including Christians, with regard to Mary in the Church as a whole. Devotion to Mary in the Orthodox traditions rests in three considerations.

First, Mary is honoured because she brought the incarnate Word of God to birth in her womb. Through her faith and obedience – her *fiat* to the will of God – Mary became the *Theotokos*, the God-bearer. I mentioned earlier that Orthodox spirituality is strongly incarnational. It is rooted in the fusion of heaven and earth: of the ordinary and the extraordinary, the divine and the human, the cosmic and the earthed. Mary is iconic in this respect through the fusion of the human with the divine in the genetic make-up of the Christ child. Mary's willing participation in the Christ event brings about the mystical birth that made possible life-saving death and resurrection.

Secondly, Mary is inspirational in the sense that, by the indwelling of the Holy Spirit, we are all *Theotokos*: we are all God-bearers and know within ourselves the fusion of the divine and the human. We recognise that through us, God gives birth to the kingdom.

Thirdly, in Orthodox spirituality, Mary is the archetypical human being, representing as she does the fragility and vulnerability of us all and of the fallenness of humanity. At the same time she represents the hope of our calling to faithfulness and the wonder of a God who would stoop to enter human life in its ordinariness, transfiguring our ordinariness into something exquisite and extraordinary. Rowan Williams offers a deeper reflection of the iconic relationship between the Christ child and Mary as representational of the relationship between God and humanity in his book *Ponder These Things*.[107]

The Iconographical tradition

Mention of the iconic figure of Mary brings us to the fifth feature of Orthodox spirituality that I would like us to reflect upon: icons. Icons are sacred images which evoke devotion and draw us into a spiritual experience with God. They are not graven images to be worshipped. They seek to convey the heavenly as well as the ordinary. Icons are visible teaching aids and have a long history of bringing the truths of the Christian faith to countless people, particularly those who could not read. Once we have learned something of the language of an icon, its depths begin to be revealed. However, we can take a lifetime and still learn something new about God or insights into how we might respond to God, simply by staying prayerfully with an icon.

107. R. Williams (2002), *Ponder These Things*, The Canterbury Press.

Icons are more than religious works of art, yet paintings can show relationship symbolically. Portraits of Queen Elizabeth I, for example, were not so much designed to show her likeness as to show some attribute of her, her authority or her power. Designs of eyes and ears strewn across her gown referred to her awareness and knowledge of what her subjects were up to. A string of pearls was a pictorial reference to her virginity. A red rose reminded her people of her place in the Tudor dynasty. A fan indicated hot weather and gloves suggested cold weather. Seen in the same portrait they suggested that she was queen of the elements. Her shape was distorted to flatter or to make her appear more grand. No one expects people to worship the painting (or even the monarch depicted). The depiction is representational. Religious icons are full of symbolism, some of it profoundly theological.

Icons are written, not drawn! An iconographer may take months or years to prayerfully write an icon. They are earthly creations using wood and paint; the very materials represent the things of the earth, whilst gold leaf and rich paint evoke the glory of heaven. Figures in icons may show the fusion of God and humanity: fallen and broken humanity juxtaposed with divine mercy and grace.

In an icon nothing is accidental: the tiniest detail has meaning. Relative sizes of figures are not meant to be proportional in any human representational way. For example, a thick throat in human physiological terms looks like a goitre, but in iconography a thick throat tells us that the person depicted is filled with the Holy Spirit: the *pneuma* or breath of the Holy Spirit is ready to burst from them in praise or prophecy. Colours, gestures, postures and eye direction all have deep meaning.

If the reader is new to iconographic spirituality I suggest they begin with an icon written by Andrei Rublev around AD 1360. It is an icon of the Holy Trinity based on the story of the three visitors to Abraham in Genesis 18. This icon is rich in symbolism. The shape of the circle represents unity, perfection and love. One can read, too, the octagon: a symbol dating back to the earliest times as Christians recalled the six days of creation, the seventh day of rest plus the day of resurrection. Early Byzantine churches were built in an octagonal way, and octagonal baptismal fonts are not uncommon. The three figures in Rublev's icon represent the persons of the Trinity, their clothes and the background to them giving clues as to their identity

One could spend a lifetime with this icon and still find something new in it. To pray with this icon is to be drawn to it not as painted wood, but to be drawn deeper into a relationship with the Triune God.

As this was the starting point for this reflection on Orthodox spirituality it seems appropriate to close on a Trinitarian note.

The Charismatic tradition: Being shaped by the Spirit who is Life

Can I move seamlessly from the Orthodox tradition to the Charismatic tradition? I believe so! Presence, power and participation in the Divine Life are also part of the Charismatic spirituality legacy. Disposition to be within reach of the Divine is fused with expectation that such an encounter will change us and others: that we will become more like God, being and acting in the name of the all-powerful God, revealed in his Majestic Son and experienced through the Holy Paraclete. We remember that we live by the breath of God, the *pneuma* of the Spirit. Where the Spirit is present the power of the Spirit is at work in and through us. We are made alive, regenerated, by the Spirit, and the same Spirit is at work in the Church, reshaping our identity – shaping us to become more like Christ.

We should not assume that the Spirit is restricted by the Church and its view of itself; nor is it inhibited by internal wrangling or disputes, by the fractional nature of denominational difference. Neither should we assume that the scope of God's Spirit is co-terminus with the boundaries of the Church universal. The Spirit blows where she wills![108] For the purpose of this reflection it is sufficient, however, if we hold that through God's people the world is reshaped and the kingdom of God is established and that each of us is a unique creation of God, crafted, shaped, nourished and empowered by God's Spirit at work in and through us. Central to our unique spirituality 'fragrance' will be our desire to live by the Spirit as we allow ourselves to be drawn to the vast heart of the Father's love through union with our Lord Jesus Christ.

For these reasons we cannot consider the Charismatic tradition as just another tasty morsel on the smorgasbord of Christian spirituality, to be tasted and rejected as not our kind of thing. We are all charismatic because we have all been graced by the Holy Spirit and have charisms – gifts of God's grace given to us for prayer, given to us to enable us to speak out in God's name for the furtherance of God's kingdom and so that we can be channels of God's healing love for the world.

Ever since the Holy Spirit was given to the Church on the Day of Pentecost, Christians have exercised the gifts they

---

108. John 3:8.

have been given. From time to time there has a been a wave of renewal of the Holy Spirit: perhaps not so much a seasonal gust of wind and then a season of calm as God's people noticing the work of the Spirit or remembering the gifts the Spirit brings. There was one such wave of renewal in the late nineteenth century: a wave that crossed existing denominational boundaries but which caused so much divided opinion that those who had recognised the Spirit's power were forced to leave their own denominational roots and find each other. Out of that renewal came the Pentecostal churches.

Another wave swept the globe in the 1970s, bringing renewal which largely survived its critics and sceptics so that Christians of all denominations were touched by it and, in finding one another, did not break away but helped to repair something of the brokenness and to foster a spirit of celebration of diversity within the Christian Church universal.

There are others better able than I am to expound on this subject. My purpose is to encourage the reader to be receptive to the God whose Spirit dwells with us and whose gifting brings shape to our spirituality through the charisms of the Spirit. For the purposes of this reflection on the charismatic tradition I want to offer a brief note about two of the charisms commonly to be found in the Church: speaking in tongues and prophecy.

Tongues

Do you think speaking in tongues is commonly to be found among God's people? You might say that it is not! I would say it is the best-kept secret in the Church! I meet so many Christians who shyly admit to tongues featuring in their prayer, though many are not bold enough (or do not see the need) to use their gift publicly.

For the purpose of this reflection I would like the reader to consider how, in prayer, one can be stuck for words to express our deepest feelings – whether to adore God or to express deep gratitude for all that God has done for us or for others. We might come before God with someone or a circumstance on our heart but we are unsure how to pray about the situation. Here the gift of tongues comes to the rescue so that we can pray from our heart without known words getting in the way. St Paul says, 'Likewise the Spirit helps us in our weakness; for we do not know how to pray as we ought, but that very Spirit intercedes with sighs too deep for words.'[109]

For me, tongues is a love language. Like any love language it can sound strange or silly to anyone other than the lover and the beloved. Tongues is Spirit-inspired language and can be helpful for us to express ourselves in our loving relationship with God. St Paul teaches, 'Be filled with the Spirit, as you sing psalms and hymns and spiritual songs among yourselves, singing and making melody to the Lord in your hearts'.[110]

I would also encourage the reader to make the connection between the gift of tongues and the gift of silent prayer, since both move us beyond verbal limitations to express to God all that is in our heart. Somewhere between tongues and silence is the sigh 'too deep for words'. A sigh expresses so much: yearning, longing, sorrow, joy, grief, satisfaction, and its value in prayer is not to be underestimated.

---

109. Romans 8:26.
110. Ephesians 5:18b, 19.

Prophecy

Thanks to the popular appeal of pier-end fortune tellers, the notion of prophecy is largely misunderstood. In the Christian tradition it is not about foretelling so much as forth-telling. It is a way in which God speaks to us and to the world, bringing God's message of love and mercy, and guiding us into all truth.

To be considered authentic, a word of prophecy needs to accord with everything else we know of how God wants us to live or behave. For example, if a member of our congregation tells us that God has spoken to them and is telling the community that in order to solve their financial difficulties they should rob a bank, no one in the congregation would be able to affirm that the 'word' that person had received was from God because the instruction to rob a bank would be to act against God's law. Prophecies need to be affirmed by others. We discern the Lord's will for us together as well as alone. Foster reminds us, 'The Spirit bestows gifts of discernment and prophecy to guide the life of the community.'[111]

Prophecy is also the gift of speaking out in boldness in order to draw attention to injustice or discrimination. One thinks of Martin Luther King and his great prophetic speeches. Speaking prophetically has, in all of history, caused Christians to risk and, sometimes, to lose their lives.

In this chapter we have moved at breakneck speed through three major traditions in the Church: the Contemplative tradition, the Orthodox tradition and the Charismatic tradition. These are just three traditions which continue to shape Christian spirituality and which demonstrate how we

111. R. J. Foster, *Streams of Living Water*, p.129.

129

encounter God in presence, power and participation in the Divine Life.

Ending this chapter on the gift of prophecy and the message of God for the world turns our reflections from our individual encounters with God and our corporate spirituality of belonging in the Church to our interface with the world, with all creation and to lifestyle choices, all of which also shape our spirituality. These are the themes of the next chapter.

CHAPTER SIX

Spirituality and the outward journey

In earlier chapters we considered how we have been shaped by life events and circumstances as well as by the God of love who, through grace and the working of the Holy Spirit, is transforming us into Christlikeness. In this chapter we consider how we, ourselves, shape our spirituality by the life choices we make and by participation in, and cooperation with, God's mission of love to the world. As individuals, as members of the Body of Christ and as members of the human race we play our part in transforming the world. Whether this is through life-fulfilling vocation or by contributing to good causes, we help to make a difference. Authentic spirituality requires that the 'inside' of us – our spiritual aspirations and our prayerful practice – matches the 'outside' of us – the way we live and behave towards others. If the inside and the outside do not match, we are in danger of living a life of smug self-service and hypocrisy. Unless we embrace the world in love, our spirituality becomes pietistic and self-indulgent.

If we are honest, the inside and the outside of us do not match well a lot of the time. We need to be realistic and not too hard on ourselves, but we should regularly review how we live in relation to other people, to the environment, to addiction, preoccupation or obsession. We review how our lifestyle impacts upon the lifestyle of our neighbour. This exercise can include everything from our responsibility to the conservation of the environment (such as recycling our waste or minimising our carbon footprint) to whether the clothes we wear and the food we eat are ethically sourced.

Spirituality and creation

In previous chapters we have reflected on how we relate to God and how we are inspired and sustained in our relationship. We have owned that, as members together of the Body of Christ, we relate to God in community as well as individually. A healthy spirituality depends not only on our disposition or ability to relate to God but our disposition to and engagement with the world around us. Even cloistered religious maintain an awareness of the world beyond the cloister and offer prayer, night and day, for the world and its needs. If there is no engagement with the world, our pious practices can so easily become self-indulgent or vacuous.

One way in which our inward journey to the heart of God is balanced with our outward journey to find God in the world around us is through the inspiration of creation. Which of us has not been moved, at one time or another, by a beautiful vista: perhaps a mountain range or a rolling meadow, a seascape or a single bloom in a garden? Inspiration in creation comes to us in so many ways as we behold one another: in beauty, character, gifting, humour, affection and love. It comes as we hold with one fingertip the tiny hand of a newborn child. The untamed nature of creation is awesome, too, as witnessed in stormy seas beating against the shore or in the drama of thunder and lightning.

Inspirational poetry

The works of the nineteenth-century English poet John Clare are enjoying something of a renaissance. It may be that Clare's love of God in creation together with his mental illness make for a more real understanding and relationship between Creator and created. The very syntactical abrasions in the text tell us not only of Clare's educational inadequacies but of his inner turmoil. His poetry, at times, puts one in mind of the painting *The Scream* by Edvard Munch. The use of clashing colours is offensive to the eye but adds to the drama of the piece. There are parallels, too, in music: a contemporary example might be the anguish in some of Tchaikovsky's works. The juxtaposition of artistic expression and a tortured mind can produce inspirational works which prevent creation being subsumed to sentimentalism. Clare lived in a part of rural England that can be considered bleak, even depressing, in wintertime, yet the open but flattish land and the big skies offer a freedom and a loftiness of thought. Clare thrived in such an environment and felt closest to God walking in the open countryside; he was sorely inhibited in spirit by the ensuing 'enclosures' laws. Some might say that Clare wasn't a Christian but rather a Unitarian worshipping God as Creator. Nevertheless, Clare's poems reveal his love of God in creation.

Clare is but one example of how creation affects spirituality; we have a long tradition of inspirational material in praise of God as Creator. The canticle, *Benedicite*, for example, traditionally said or sung as part of the office of Morning Prayer, offers us expression of our deep gratitude for God's creation and all that it tells us about God in untamed majesty as well as in generous provision of the fruits of the earth. Likewise our hymnology has much to offer. The words of a hymn by Mrs C. F. Alexander – 'All things bright and beautiful' – have inspired a number of generations. Her style, often now thought of as outdated, was of a fashion common to many in England in the early part of the nineteenth century. Like John Clare, Mrs Alexander was influenced by the religious and social conditioning of her time. The works of the contemporary poet, Mary Oliver, also focus on God in creation but with a very different feel to either Clare or Mrs Alexander.

Poetry has much to offer in the way of spiritual nourishment. Sometimes it is simply a matter of finding a poet with whom one resonates and whose work expresses something we find difficult to articulate. As we turn from ourselves to the needs of others, poetry can inform us of the worldview of others and help us to empathise with them. Would poems about the open countryside appeal to someone who lives in a densely populated area, whose job keeps them rooted in a town and whose recreation is limited? Would it appeal to the agoraphobic or the chronically depressed whose only view from their home is across rooftops? Clare's 'last words', written in 1842 from the confines of a mental asylum, in the poem, 'I am', epitomise the articulation of creational spirituality in poetry. The final verse runs:

I long for scenes where man has never trod;
a place where woman never smiled or wept;
there to abide with my creator, God,
and sleep as I in childhood sweetly slept;
untroubling and untroubled where I lie
the grass below or above the vaulted sky.[112]

Poetry as a spirituality resource can give articulation to deep aspiration and inspiration, not only of our personal situation but in our prayerful concern for the needs of the world.

Spirituality and world awareness

World awareness, in both the joy and heartbreak of creation, is the antidote to pietistic self-indulgence, but it is only the

---

112. 'I am' from J. Clare (2007), John Clare: Selected by Paul Farley, London: Faber and Faber Ltd, p.113.

SPIRITUALITY AND THE OUTWARD JOURNEY

beginning. We begin to understand what the Apostle James meant when he said, 'Faith without works is barren'.[113]

We may feel helpless in the face of a world crisis, yet even the tiniest donation to an appropriate aid agency can make a difference. If nothing more, we can bring the matter to God in prayer: not in a way whereby we read to God the *Nine O'clock News* in the assumption that God has no idea of the latest tragedy to befall, nor in a way that tells God what should be done about it, but in a way which stands with God and helps to open the conduits of grace, mercy and peace which are God's gifts to the world. Standing thus with God, on a regular basis, with the needs of the world on our heart, we will find that our world awareness increases. In addition, we will more readily engage with the needs of the world, finding human and God-given ways to make a difference in the lives of others. Our attitude to creation will move from awesome marvelling through inspiration in prayer to a desire to conserve all that God has given. Further, we will want more readily to bring water to desert places, food to the hungry and shelter to the homeless, the displaced and the refugee. Deeply inspired, nourished and equipped in our inner journey, we will travel the outward journey seeking the face of Christ in the poor, the destitute, the perpetrator and the victim of crime, abuse or neglect. Awareness of the world and its needs, together with the Gospel imperatives,[114] will change our lifestyle.

Spirituality and lifestyle

Guidance on how we are to live is written in the Holy Scriptures. From the Ten Commandments[115] to the Sermon

---

113. James 2:20.
114. Matthew 25:31-46
115. Exodus 20.

on the Mount,[116] we have guidelines, but we will also face challenges as we seek to live a holy and a wholesome life. Contemporary situations bring knotty ethical dilemmas that take time, prayer, thought, compassion and love to resolve or at least to hold without prejudice or judgement as we, together with others, work them through in the light of a deepening comprehension of the complexity of human nature. Some of our prejudices pre-date the Christ event, and other prejudices have been engendered, historically, by Christians and in the name of Christ!

Engagement in ethical and moral dilemmas may not be something we feel able to do in any major or robust way. We are not all called to be members of Parliament. Not all of us feel called to march through the streets waving banners, but on a daily basis each one of us is called upon to make a choice. It may be whether or not to buy something that has not been ethically sourced, it may be the moment of choice when we walk past a beggar in the street, or it may be a matter of whether or not we leave the television on standby rather than switching it off to save electricity.

Deep relational engagement with God cannot be a hallmark of a healthy spirituality unless that deep engagement changes us, even by a small degree at a time. An authentic spirituality will be evidenced in lifestyle. Once again, we look to the fruit of the Spirit[117] for evidence of our conformity to Christ: an outcome of both the grace of God at work in us and our own efforts to live authentically, holy and wholly before God. Do not let the reader imagine that I think this is an easy matter! So many challenges assail us, and we continually fall short, but by the grace and mercy of God we can turn

---

116. Matthew 5–7.
117. Galatians 5:22-3.

again and again in the direction of Christ, not out of fear of punishment for getting it wrong but out of love for God and deep gratitude for God's infinite love for us all. Perseverance will carry us far. Perhaps Hannah's story might encourage us.

Hannah's story

Hannah was more than 100 years of age when she died. Into her late nineties she lived alone in a bungalow and took good care of herself. She had a deep faith and welcomed the sacrament of Holy Communion in her home every month. Unable to leave the bungalow very often, Hannah was nevertheless well informed not only about happenings in the village but also about happenings around the world. When a visitor arrived, Hannah would reach for the remote control to switch off the television. She would make coffee in the microwave after she had received Holy Communion and would want to sit and discuss the events that had been brought to her attention by the media.

Hannah had lived through two world wars and through the ongoing threat of nuclear war. She was concerned about global terrorism and about the effect of viral illnesses of many kinds: pandemics of this and that. She was aware of earthquakes, tsunamis, floods and fires. She understood herself to be living on a volatile globe spinning in a universe. She understood human vulnerability but she did not regard herself as unduly vulnerable. She trusted in God for her safety. She lived as faithfully as she could, sustained and nourished by the Holy Scriptures and the sacraments of the New Covenant, and she knew the love of God in neighbours and friends. She had worked in the service of a grand house from the age of 14 until she retired at the age of 72. In retirement she worked in support of local charities and had raised funds for an international charity. She lived frugally (more by necessity than intent!) and could be fiercely independent. She could be caustic and outspoken and had very definite political views. She lived life to the fullest her circumstances would allow. She would say of herself that she was content and, in latter years, was more than ready to meet her Maker and Redeemer. Hannah modelled authentic spirituality. She travelled the inward journey and the outward journey.

Going the extra mile

At the heart of all Christian spirituality traditions is the desire to live more fully, more completely, a Christocentric life: to model ourselves on both the teaching and the example of Jesus Christ in conformity to the will of God. Wholehearted response to Christ, perhaps out of gratitude for all he did for us in his death and rising, means seeking to model our life upon his. Foster suggests that our ultimate goal is

> to ever deepen formation of the inner personality so as to reflect the glory and the goodness of God: an ever more radiant conformity to the life of faith and desires and habits of Jesus; an utter transformation of our creatureliness into whole and perfect sons and daughters of God.[118]

This desire for wholehearted commitment to Christ came to me in my late teens when I sought entry to a religious community. When asked to sum up why I thought I should give my life to the service of God and God's people, my response came not directly from Holy Scripture but from the final two lines of the Isaac Watts hymn, 'When I survey

---

118. R. J. Foster, *Streams of Living Water*, p.85.

the wondrous cross', in the lines 'Love so amazing, so divine, demands my soul, my life my all.'[119]

A wholehearted response to Christ's invitation to live his risen life has, for many throughout history, been formalised in vows in accordance with the so-called 'Evangelical Counsels' of 'poverty' (perfect charity), 'chastity' (right relationships) and 'obedience'. Living according to these precepts, with or without a vow on the matter, are not the exclusive province of monks and nuns. They are for any who would deepen their identity with Christ and would model their lifestyle on him.

The call to live according the Evangelical Counsels is rooted in the Gospels and is an invitation rather than a command. This is important to remember because it ensures that we don't feel driven to a lifestyle out of fear of the consequences of not living life in a certain way and so that we don't draw ourselves back into pietistic introspection. Our voluntary engagement with the Counsels must not become a stick we have sharpened to poke ourselves with! Living according the Evangelical Counsels (or aspiring to do so) is as much about a shift in attitude as it is about a change of lifestyle, though the one feeds the other.

The roots of the Evangelical Counsels, as the name implies, are to be found in the Holy Gospels. Through them, Jesus Christ, the Emmanuel, the God-made-man, speaks to us in words of encouragement. His words come to us through stories of his encounter with others. Sometimes they ask the questions we would like to ask ourselves. Jesus' response to his interlocutors is his response to us, too.

I would like to offer further reflections on the Evangelical Counsels through the lens of Franciscan spirituality. The

---

119. I. Watts, 'When I survey the wondrous cross', 1707. Public domain.

counsels are by no means exclusive to Franciscanism but the outworking of them does draw us towards an outward journey in spirituality that embraces the world and its needs which is at the heart of Franciscan spirituality.

Franciscan spirituality

Arguably, St Francis of Assisi is among the best known and best loved of the saints, but what might be his appeal? Perhaps it is the way he models complete and utter commitment to Christ, to a lifestyle we might all emulate. For some it is his love of creation. All these things are worthy of note.

We should not neglect St Francis' spiritual sister, St Clare (1181–1226) and all that she, too, models in Christian discipleship. The total commitment of both stands in stark contrast to their life and times. Their simple yet profound action of stripping themselves of possessions, exclusive relationships and attachments, together with their submission to the authority of the Church, would have caused many a good-hearted woman and man to consider their own lifestyle and discipleship. At the centre of their spirituality is Jesus Christ and his birth, Passion, death and rising. The intricate and beautiful interplay between their devotion to the sufferings of Christ for our sake and their profound joy is intriguing, attractive, accessible in its simplicity and alluring in its profundity.

The essence of Francis and Clare continues to pervade the atmosphere of worldwide Christendom, and its followers in the Franciscan tradition continue to contribute to the mission of the Church in joy-filled service and simplicity of lifestyle.

The Evangelical Counsels: poverty

The invitation of Jesus to a deeper relationship and

commitment to becoming Christlike is clear in relation to the evangelical counsel of 'poverty' from the words of Jesus to the rich young man recorded in St Matthew's Gospel: 'If you wish to be perfect, go, sell your possessions, and give the money to the poor, and you will have treasure in heaven; then come, follow me.'[120]

Let us reflect on this text in context. The rich young man in the Gospel asks what he should do to obtain eternal life, and Jesus tells him to 'keep the commandments.' Note that Jesus differentiates between 'entering into life' and another (voluntary) depth of commitment which Jesus invites the young man to consider, since he seems to want a deeper commitment than that to which he is already committed. So when the young man presses further, Jesus tells him, 'If you wish to be perfect, go, sell your possessions, and give the money to the poor, and you will have treasure in heaven; then come, follow me.'

It is from this passage that the term 'counsel for perfection' comes, although some translators from the original Greek offer, 'If you would be complete' rather than 'perfect', which the reader may find more attractive. Would you aspire to being 'perfect' or would you aspire to being 'complete'? Consider the thoughts, feelings and memories evoked by each of those words. Does either inspire you to change your lifestyle? We may want to ask how relevant or realistic is this counsel in our time and culture.

Barry and Jean's story

Barry tells the story of how, following a burglary at home (one in which his wife and he encountered the burglar as he

---

120. Matthew 19:16-22, especially verse 21.

fled from the house!), Barry asked the policeman if the burglar was likely to return now that he knew they had 'stuff'. '"Stuff"!' the policeman exclaimed. 'No, he won't return because you have "stuff", because everybody has "stuff" and, with respect, you have no more "stuff" than anyone else in these parts!'

The incident did change Barry and Jean's relationship to their 'stuff', however. Although the burglar got away with very little, it was the thought of him in the house and of what he might have taken that was of real personal and sentimental value to Barry and Jean that gave them pause for thought, rather than what constituted 'stuff'. Possessions can take quite a bit of looking after in terms of time and money. Investments in shares or property can be absorbing and can become a full-time job if they are considerable. Such time and attention given to possessions can constitute the *love* of money of which Paul writes to Timothy, 'The love of money is a root of all kinds of evil.'[121]

Preoccupation with wealth, or with anything else for that matter, can distract us from paying attention to God or to the needs of our neighbour. We may ask ourselves if we have such a preoccupation and whether or not it is in that preoccupation that we have our emotional, spiritual or material 'treasure'.

Jesus brings a vision of a world where poverty is no more. We can easily understand why he wants this: God has provided enough so that no one should be hungry or thirsty for clean water. God desires a world of wholesome nourishment for all with shelter from the elements and safety from danger. Greed and selfishness, self-serving politicians and those who exploit the most vulnerable in the world are among those

---

121. 1 Timothy 6:10.

responsible for an unfair distribution of even the basics of food, water or medicines.

For all the most obvious reasons, Jesus does not advocate that we live in abject poverty, but there is a reason which is not so apparent. In the way that riches can distract us because they require so much attention in their acquisition, protection and maintenance, so abject poverty brings similar distractions. When hunger pains and despair of how to feed one's family are a constant preoccupation, it can be argued that there is no personal resource left to engage more deeply with God or our wider neighbour. The American psychologist Abraham Maslow (1908–1970), who was best known for creating a hierarchy of needs, argued that we cannot aspire to wider, deeper or fuller aspirations of life until basic needs are met,[122] although we could respond that the poor cry out to God with more sincerity than the over-fed and that courage, sacrifice and acts of heroism fuelled by despair or anger at injustice have changed societies.

The Lord's invitation to 'holy poverty' is not a call to abject, gut-wrenching poverty but rather an invitation to a life that will not be characterised by preoccupation either with worrying where the next meal is to come from or with worrying about how the investments are doing. It will be a life where there is sufficient to set us free to love God and our neighbour as ourselves. This will be characterised by living according to what we need rather than according to what we want. By this lifestyle choice, many of us will find we have more than we need and may be inspired to share our excess with those who have a greater need. Some readers may already set aside a tithe of their income for the benefit of

---

122. Maslow's theory was expounded fully in A. H. Maslow (1954), *Motivation and Personality*, New York: Harper.

others, though it can be argued that ten per cent of very little can be the difference between making ends meet and not so doing, whereas ten per cent of a fortune would not be missed and is the equivalent of tossing a coin casually into a collection plate.

The Evangelical Counsels: chastity

Francis of Assisi and his spiritual sister Clare are excellent examples of a wholehearted response to the counsel of holy poverty modelled as an out-living of wholehearted commitment to following Christ. They are also excellent examples of a wholehearted response to the counsel of 'holy chastity'. They remained detached from exclusive human relations in order to be free to love not only all God's people but all of God's creation. But was it a vow of chastity or was it celibacy that set them free? It is very easy to confuse the two. The scriptural warrant for this counsel comes from texts such as Matthew 19:12 where Jesus spoke of 'eunuchs who have made themselves eunuchs for the kingdom of heaven' and added, 'Let anyone accept this who can.'

Perhaps those words of Jesus influenced Paul's opinion on the value of celibacy. St Paul has much to say about the sins of the flesh and about faithfulness in marriage, and he gives the impression that, in his opinion, the single state is to be preferred over marriage. Paul expected the imminent return of Christ to whisk all his people off to heaven where celibacy and the married state would have no relevance, so single people might as well stay single (and therefore celibate) and the married members of the community should remain faithful in marriage. This teaching has coloured the view of celibacy and the married state ever since, and has created no end of problems for those who would minister in Christ's name but have no freedom to marry should they so desire. The danger was that the Evangelical Counsels, implied and taught by the apostles, were considered not so much as voluntarily going the extra mile in discipleship and in pursuit of perfection (or completion) but were to be considered *incumbent* on Christians: an obligation to be observed, with dire consequences for those who failed to comply.

In a contemporary inclusive society this is hard to justify, if chastity is considered commensurate with celibacy. The counsel of chastity is, however, much more than a call to celibacy. Celibacy is not to be discounted as the pathway for some in the pursuit of wholehearted conformity to Christ, but neither is it to be implied that a sexual relationship within an exclusive partnership where there is declared intention of being together for life is a less high calling or is less holy.

Chastity means honouring the personhood of others; it is about right relationships. Right relationships means not abusing or exploiting another. I would add that taking another person for granted is a failing in holy chastity. Following this train of thought, one could hold that anything that makes another feel degraded or less of a person is a failing in chastity. This begs the question: what, in our society today, might be the particular challenges to living a 'chaste' life?

The Evangelical Counsels: obedience

Once again we have before us St Francis and St Clare who model the counsel of obedience, but where is the scriptural warrant for this counsel? We could consider Romans 13:1: 'Let every person be subject to the governing authorities; for there is no authority except from God'. The whole chapter bears reading in this respect. For gospel authority we consider the words of Jesus in relation to doing God's will, or the clever response under pressure that we should render to Caesar the things that are Caesar's.[123] More than words are the actions of Jesus who, as St Paul reminds us, 'became obedient to the point of death – even death on a cross.'[124] One aspect of the Counsel of obedience has to be death to self in order that we might live for Christ.

We also have a model of servanthood. We recall that iconic moment when Jesus washed the feet of his disciples and taught them that they should so serve one another.[125]

The Evangelical Counsel of obedience can be better understood if we go back to the root of the word 'obedience', which means 'to listen'. We have reflected in a previous chapter on St Benedict's legacy and of his Rule, the prologue of which begins with an injunction to listen. In later chapters of the Rule, Benedict offers instruction to those who are called to hold positions of leadership in the community. Once again he calls them to listen to the community: to take into account the views and opinions of others so that through mutual listening God's will may be discerned. Obedience is mutual accountability and includes hearing and respecting the view of others.

This is a far cry from some of the models of obedience in the history of the Church. Far too often, obedience has meant the unconditional acceptance of anything anyone in authority wishes to impose, laying all open to inhuman treatment, exploitation and abuse. Equally, those under obedience can easily abdicate all responsibility for even the

---

123. Matthew 22:21.
124. Philippians 2:8.
125. John 13:3-12.

smallest of decisions in daily living, rendering themselves disabled and, ultimately, a burden on the community.

One cannot separate out the Counsels of poverty, chastity and obedience from one another except for a brief exercise such as this in order to explore basic principles because, in reality, the Counsels together make for a framework for growth into conformity to Christ: each interplaying with the others.

Those who live in community under vows of poverty, chastity and obedience continually assess and review their lifestyle by listening to one another's views on how resources might best be used and on how relationships might be improved so that God-given gifts might best be used for the glory of God and in the furtherance of the mission of the Church. It should be said that all communities have their tensions and disagreements, sometimes exhibiting spectacularly unchristian behaviour! Vows are one thing, living them out, quite another!

Church communities and congregations adopt similar methods of assessment and review, sharing wisely all they have in God's service (poverty), striving for right relationships within the community (chastity) and listening to one another (obedience) as they continually re-evaluate their mission under God.

This is good practice, but are these Counsels for perfection? Yes, of course, but they are not, in themselves, counsels for *perfectionism*, which can be more about pride than the kingdom of God. Rather, as in Matthew 5:48, 'Be perfect, therefore, as your heavenly Father is perfect.'

I asked Sister Helen Julian of the Anglican Franciscan Community of St Francis what drew her to Franciscanism.

Sister Helen Julian's story

I became a Franciscan not because I was attracted to Francis, but because I met Franciscans. A weekend at a friary in Northumberland left me intrigued and challenged by a life which seemed to hold together prayer and community and work and a very earthed kind of joy. I came away thinking, 'I want to be part of this in some way.' As I made repeat visits and got to know the brothers better, I realised that it wasn't as straightforward as I'd first thought; there were demands and difficulties and struggles under the surface. But the vision of a life 'lived whole' in the footsteps of Francis, and of Clare, the first Franciscan woman, who I later came to value highly, kept drawing me on. After 28 years in community myself I know only too well the demands and struggles, but I also know that Franciscanism (not a word Francis would have liked!) contains resources to sustain the whole of life, whatever the context in which it's lived.

Franciscanism and a world-changing spirituality

I asked Sister Helen Julian in what ways can Franciscanism be world changing. She responded:

The Franciscan vision of the world is a challenging one. The popular picture of Francis as the saint of the birdbath and the bunny rabbit is only a small part of a much bigger picture, in which everything and everybody is part of one family, brother and sister to one another. This requires a relationship with our brothers and sisters in other parts of the world, and with every part of creation, which treats them as we would members of our own family. It's a view which challenges our natural tendency to close down our vision and to restrict our compassion.

It would seem impossibly demanding if it wasn't for another part of the Franciscan vision – that of the unbounded generosity of God. Francis saw God as the great giver, and learned to depend totally on God for all that he needed. This is where his love of poverty came from, not from a hatred of the material world, or a rejection of the good things of life. Living with open hands he saw whatever he had as gifts to be shared, and his trust in God led to a deep and real joy even in times of sickness and difficulty.

Franciscans have broken down barriers between Church denominations and have materially changed the lives of millions through their work with the poor and the destitute. Many of their members, both women and men, have been martyred for their faith.

For those unable to live either in an enclosed religious community (such as the Poor Clares) or in community in a myriad of settings throughout the world, there is a way of identifying with them, living the Franciscan way of life in a way that suits their circumstances: a way given to the world by St Francis himself. It is the Third Order, or the Tertiary commitment. It brings with it a structured prayer life that is tailored to circumstances and soaked in the central principles of Christian discipleship, and simplicity of life.

Franciscans have truly gone into all the world to 'make disciples of all nations'.[126] Although Franciscan spirituality is characterised by the inward journey towards intimate union with God through prayer, it is essentially outward looking. Franciscans today champion not only the cause of the poor and the dispossessed, the outcast and the marginalised, but also the cause of conservation of the environment as they continue in the spirit of their founders in their delight in God in creation. The sufferings of Christ and the sufferings of humanity motivate their apostleship, the aim of which is to leave the world a better place for bringing Christ's healing to the world.

126. Matthew 28:19.

In these reflections I hold Franciscan spirituality as just one example of the richness of Christian spirituality heritage which engages with the world and its needs and the part we are all called to play in God's mission to the world. In the previous chapter we acknowledged that it is by God's saving grace that we enjoy an intimate relationship with God and that we are energised by God's love for us and for the whole world. Here we explore how by showing love and mercy, through the reception of grace and a disposition of gratitude, we are re-energised and how we re-energise others as we share something of God's love for all. In this, the energy of Franciscanism is inspirational among many robust and passionate traditions in the Church.

The Five Marks of Mission

Here I think it would be useful to our reflection on the outward journey in spirituality to consider what we understand to be the mission of the Church. The Five Marks of Mission was developed by the Anglican Consultative Council between 1984 and 1990. It is generally accepted among Anglicans, though it may well resonate with Christians of other denominations too as summarising all that we feel we are called to do for the furtherance of the kingdom of God.

The Five Marks of Mission from a spirituality perspective

First Mark. First and foremost we remember that the mission of the Church is the mission of Christ himself.[127] It is Christ who said that when he was lifted up (either on the cross or into heaven), he would draw all people to himself. As members of the Body of Christ we are Christ's presence in

---

127. John 12:32.

the world, and we play our part in the drawing of all people to God. This was important to St Francis too, who allegedly told his followers to 'Preach the Word of God' adding the rider, 'Use words if necessary.' This should bring great comfort to those who still understand spreading the good news of the kingdom and making disciples of all the nations as solely a matter of 'door-stepping' or standing on a box in the market place! St Francis reminds us that the way we live, even before we speak of the kingdom, will draw others to Christ. Introverts take heart!

Second Mark. We are to teach, baptise and nurture new believers. Again, we can teach by example as well as through traditional and modern teaching methods. Sharing the experience of both our inward journey and our outward journey into Christ can 'speak' and inspire others. We are not all going to be baptisers of new believers but we can support those who are and participate in the preparation of others for baptism. We can be more faithful godparents and make an effort to welcome seekers and those exploring faith as well as to welcome the newly baptised into the community of the Church. Holding in prayer all those involved is the least we can do, but it is nonetheless very important.

Third Mark. An equally important aspect of our mission is to seek to transform unjust structures of society, to challenge violence of every kind and to pursue peace and reconciliation. I am reminded of one inner-city church where the small but faithful congregation were so used to coming and going to church on Sunday mornings that they failed to notice the build-up around the cartilage of the church building of vagrants and those addicted to alcohol or drugs. The congregants had become a 'holy huddle', detached

LIFE SHAPING SPIRITUALITY

from the needs of their neighbour. It took a new parish priest to wake them up to the plight on their doorstep. This same small group of churchgoers, most of them in their seventies, began to engage with the people outside the church (in every sense!) and to try to make a difference in their lives. Their many small, quiet initiatives included helping people to make sense of letters from government departments and going with individuals to speak out for them. A clothing bank was formed and a hot meal provided several times each week from the tiny kitchen at the back of the church. Their neighbour breathed new life into the congregation and, as a result, they exuded a joy they had not known. This made the church more attractive to seekers.

Fourth Mark. We are called to respond to human need by loving service. It is very easy to imagine that we are a world divided into those who serve and those who are served: that there are fixers and those who are fixed. But this is to suggest that there is a paradigm of human well-being against which we are to be measured (and found wanting). Jesus came that we might have life, and have it abundantly,[128] and we are all less than abundantly filled with his life. We all have needs. Contemporary attitudes towards disability are arguably better than they used to be, but most models still want to measure us against a perfect model: a model of their own creating. Those of us who are disabled recognise disability in others and would argue that everyone has a disability of some sort, be it physical, mental, emotional or spiritual. The mission of Christ is to bring the fullness of life to all. Our task is to look about us and to see what can be done for others to enhance the quality of their life and to be open to

---

128. John 10:10.

receive the ministry of others in bringing the fullness of Christ's life to us.

Fifth Mark. Finally, we are to strive to safeguard the integrity of creation and sustain and renew the life of the earth. Here, through our lifestyle choices, we can make a difference. This can be anything from recycling our waste to keeping the countryside code. It can range from fighting attempts to concrete over more greenfield sites to supporting initiatives to utilise sustainable fuel sources.

Subject to continual review or revision, the Five Marks of Mission can provide us with a convenient framework in relation to spirituality and guard us against pious introspection. They can encourage us to assist others in their spiritual growth as well to bring dignity to humanity and make for a better world for all.

The life-changing, world-changing dynamic at the heart of this is a dynamic of love. It is God's love for us, which spills out of the healthy spirit in returned love for God and for our neighbour. In addition to the 'tension' between the God of 'out there' and the God of 'in here', there will be a conduit of desire to embrace both the God of love and the love of one's neighbour. There will be a deep-seated care for the needs of others and a desire to share all that we have received from God: our material and spiritual gifting and riches.

Together with that striving for intimacy with God, those with a healthy spirituality will know how, or will be open to finding out how, to respond appropriately to the needs of their neighbour. How we help will depend on many things – circumstances, resources, opportunity, gifting – but a person with an authentic spirituality will have the urge to do *something* to help. Our desires will reflect God's desires, and there will be a desire to put love into action. Sheldrake reminds us that many of the spiritual greats (St Augustine, Julian of Norwich, Ignatius of Loyola) considered desire as the key to spiritual growth. He suggests, 'not all immediate yearnings unambiguously point to our deepest desires and that one . . . task of spirituality is to teach discernment'.[129] He maintains that we need a 'language' to identify an object of desire that draws us beyond the superficial, the immediate and the self-absorbed.

In those with an authentic spirituality, where the inside matches the outside and the outward journey is pursued along with the inward journey, there will be a desire to put love into action. Being in love with God will engender a deep desire to proclaim that love by word and deed. A desire to learn about and experience the nature of God and to be faithful to our baptism brings a desire to serve God in our neighbour as well as in worship. There will be a desire to transform and to be transformed into the likeness of Christ by the company we keep and by the lifestyle choices we make. Living for God entails a desire to live God's missional life. Thus we shall exude joy in all that God has created, including ourselves, and wonder at all that God is renewing in the life of the planet.

Space does not permit more than a mere acknowledgement of many other spirituality traditions which not only continue to influence the life of the Church but which are also world-changing. Some traditions in spirituality 'speak' to us because they resonate with our passions for justice, peace, the eradication of poverty and disease or the defeat of evil. These

---

129. P. Sheldrake, *Spirituality and Theology*, p.198.

include Quaker spirituality, and the spirituality of the Northumbrian and Iona communities. We should also include Celtic spirituality and the internationally acclaimed role of the Taizé community which attracts countless people, especially young people, through its apostolate of prayer, musicality and social action. All are open to being shaped by the Holy Spirit. All are moulded in God's love and all bear the hallmark of authenticity in the fruit of the Spirit.

Surrounded as we are by such treasures in spirituality, it can take time to find out whether any resonate sufficiently to deepen our own relationship with God and with our neighbour. Our own spirituality may be a heady cocktail of more than one tradition. If we are to find and retain spiritual health we must help ourselves and allow others to help us. Staying spiritually healthy is the subject of the final chapter.

CHAPTER SEVEN

Staying spiritually healthy

In earlier chapters we recognised that we can become spiritually 'stuck' or perhaps unravelled and subsequently re-ravelled so that, as a result of our life experiences, we are now a different shape: we have a new and different perspective on God, ourselves and the world around us. Through this voyage of discovery we may have learned something new about God. Our theology has changed and so our spirituality has changed. Hopefully, this has brought renewal of all that we have valued in our prayer relationship as well as opened up to us the adventure that 2000 years of spiritual heritage has to offer. We may have achieved a greater degree of insight into why and under what circumstances we can become stuck or depleted, even bored, in our relationship with God. In this chapter we consider prevention rather than cure.

Spiritual health cannot be disassociated from physical, mental or emotional health. To borrow from St Paul and his famous metaphor of the body: if one part of the body suffers, so does the rest.[130] We need not always look for major catastrophes to find evidence of this. Something as simple as not being able to pray when we are cold or tired is enough to make the point. Anger may be a better example. Being angry with someone (or with God) is a good reason to pray, and the physiological manifestations of anger do not necessarily get in the way. In the short term, anger can be energising, though we might be more comfortable calling it 'righteous indignation'! One thinks of Jesus in the Temple overturning

---

130. 1 Corinthians 12:26 (paraphrased).

the tables of the money-changers. Over a long period of time, however, anger can be very destructive to the spirit and can have physiological consequences (such as raised blood pressure).

Here we distinguish between short-term spiritual difficulties and long-term ones. In the short term we can cope with the upheaval of a mood or life events. We are remarkably resilient. There will be no lasting harm done. Even if we do believe that our relationship with God is seriously impaired or in peril we need to hold on to the belief that God is not moody, capricious or vindictive. God does not bear grudges but continues to gaze upon us with the same loving disposition as always. We have only to swallow our pride and let God catch our eye, to bathe us and restore us to 'our rightful mind'.[131] In the short term, then, no harm may be done, but in the long term we may be in danger of spiritual disintegration.

Living spiritually healthily, perhaps in the context of physical or mental ill health, brings its own challenges. Chronic pain preoccupies us. At such times we need to let the pain be our prayer, to let it speak for us, expressing our deepest emotions of fear or anxiety for ourselves and for those we love. Staying spiritually healthy, as we discovered in Chapter five, is not all about our own efforts. One meets people who live in the most horrendous of personal circumstances yet radiate love, peace and joy. God has graced such people that they bear their troubles in a way that is very inspirational. We play our part too. Living authentically and integrally, and living with ourselves in the face of our imperfections and failings, takes effort, energy and all the resources we can muster. Such

---

131. From the hymn 'Dear Lord and Father of mankind' by John Greenleaf Whittier (1872). Public domain.

resources may be depleted, and this is when we need to know how to call on others for help and not be too proud to do so. In the company of others we can more readily journey on.

We are on a journey towards God in Christ, growing in holiness. Our disposition is that of noticing what God is doing in us and through us and how we are growing more and more into the person we were created to be. We travel in the company of others, and our encounters with God and with others shape our spirituality. In others we meet Christ who speaks to us. Through others we learn ways of relating to God. Through our ministry to one another we help each other to sustain our focus, our energy and our commitment to discipleship. As we have noted previously, Jesus came that we might have life, and have it abundantly.[132] That life is incarnational: real and delicious. It is physical, mental and emotional as well as spiritual, but who will sustain us in it?

Here we consider some of the resources available to us.

Community

Even those called to a solitary way of life recognise that we belong in the communion of the faithful. St Benedict asserted that unless a person has learned to live in community they cannot become a solitary. Apart from any other consideration, to live a solitary life requires a lot of personal self-discipline, otherwise life becomes so totally unstructured that it deteriorates into total self-absorption and spiritual death. One reason why an experience of community life is valuable before embarking on the solitary life is that in community we learn so much about ourselves. Some of it we might prefer not to learn, but once living alone there is no escape from ourselves!

---

132. John 10:10.

'Community' comes in many different forms. A couple are a community of two! Family, work colleagues, the Pilates group members, the clientele at the local pub: these are all communities of which we might be members. All have something teach us about ourselves. All bring their challenges as well as their support, encouragement or enablement. The same goes for the community of the Church. We are called together by God for worship, for fellowship and for mutual support. It is important, therefore, that we are in a Church community that we can both give of ourselves, our gifts and talents, and also receive: a community where God's grace can flow in and around us, building us up for God's mission of love and reconciliation.

Brenda and Callum's story

Brenda and Callum had worshipped in their local church for several years. They had joined in enthusiastically with church events and activities alongside regular worship. The church had been a source of spiritual renewal for them. They had wanted children but none had come along. Being in the regular company of church families they were deeply conscious of their childlessness. They felt implied criticism within the congregation because they had a lovely home to offer a child and enjoyed a lifestyle that few of the family members could afford.

Under pressure, compounded by guilt, they looked into adopting a child. Eventually they were invited to foster a child with special needs with a view to adoption if everything worked out. The congregation were thrilled for them and pledged all manner of help and support. In the event, the help and support was not forthcoming. There were huge difficulties with regard to the child's needs, some of which were completely beyond Brenda and Callum's control. The child pined for her birth parents and did not settle into her new home at all.

Not only were the congregation unhelpful, but they were also hostile towards Brenda and Callum when the child had to return whence she came. Devastated and deeply hurt, Brenda and Callum distanced themselves from the Church. It would be six months before a member of the congregation visited them lamenting that there was a Brenda-and-Callum-shaped hole in the pew where they usually sat. Callum spoke for them both when he stated that as a result of the tragic experience of fostering, the resultant review of their faith and belief, and because of the way the congregation had treated them, they were no longer the same shape. Life experience had shaped their spirituality.

Eventually, Callum and Brenda found a congregation which did not judge them but accepted them for who they are (who they had become). They went on to make a great contribution to the life and mission of the Church. Sometimes it is necessary to stay put and to grow through adversity, but sometimes further growth is only possible by moving to another part of the Lord's vineyard. Although St Benedict would argue that one should stay and work through difficulties together, for some, the pain and hurt is so severe that to move on might be the only way forward, as it was for Brenda and Callum who had prayed for guidance on the matter and had sought wise counsel. In the end it was a chance encounter with another Church community that opened the door to healing and reconciliation.

Corporate worship

Joining together in worship makes a powerful statement about

Christian solidarity, but it is more than that. Worshipping with others affords God the opportunity to speak to us, to minister to us and to build us up for mission and ministry to others. In this it is good to have an open mind to different styles of corporate worship. We can find the regular attendance at the same act of worship Sunday by Sunday life giving and effective, but it does no harm, as occasion arises, to sample how other Christians worship. We may be pleasantly surprised that Sunday worship in a church or chapel of another Christian denomination has similarities to our own experience, or that we are challenged (in a good way) by liturgy which is markedly different from our own.

Holy Communion

Corporate Eucharistic worship is also a direct response to Christ's own commandment to 'Do this in remembrance of me.'[133] Through Christ's gift of himself to us in Holy Communion he ministers to us and draws us into the Godhead, nourishing, healing and renewing us. The reception of Holy Communion is an encounter with the Living God which nourishes, heals and revives our soul. We should never regard it as optional, though the frequency of reception of Holy Communion is a matter for personal discernment.

Prayer groups, cell groups, prayer triplets

We have the promise of Jesus that 'where two or three are gathered'[134] in his name, he is there in the midst of us. Spending time together with others in prayer, in silence and in ministering to one another has enormous potential for

---

133. Luke 22:19.
134. Matthew 18:20.

helping us move along if we are stuck, and for providing much needed stasis or stillness. It is a place for hearing the voice of God. It is a place for healing and to be healed.

There are many different sorts of prayer groups. Sizes vary, but they should not be so big that the shyest person is afraid to speak out or so small that they cannot be sustained if a couple of people are absent.

Cell groups are popular among clergy and often they are formed whilst the members are still in training for ministry. People speak of cell group relationships that span many decades, the members meeting up even once a year and sustained in between by telephone, Skype or email. One cell group I know of includes a weekly Ignatian Examen sent to every member by email. This form of support can help sustain a healthy spiritual life, providing accountability as well as mutual pastoral support.

Prayer triplets, as the name implies, are where three people meet to together to pray and who also pledge to prayerfully support one another wherever they are. The prayer triplet and the cell group have much in common.

Support networks

A support network might be, for some, the gathering together of a few people whom we trust to be there for us as we work through a particular project, phase or period of discernment in our discipleship. The members will be people we can rely on to be honest with us, to provide some accountability for our actions or advise us from their own experience, gifts or skills. Although such people might be 'gathered', they may also be disparate, nor need they be all of our own choosing. Those discerning a possible vocation to ordained ministry, for example, will seek and find support among family, friends, spiritual directors, congregants, vocations advisers, directors of ordinands and bishops.

There is always the danger of receiving conflicting advice. At worst this can leave us totally confused about the way ahead, but listening to conflicting advice can also help us to focus more clearly on what *we* believe to be right for us.

Support groups

Of inestimable value are those to whom we can turn at any time, not necessarily for advice but because they will ask no questions, will make no judgements and will hold us, nourish us and bathe us in unconditional love. Jesus enjoyed such a support group in the form of Mary, Martha and Lazarus at their home in Bethany.[135]

Family

Perhaps it is too obvious to cite family as among those who keep us spiritually healthy. We may recognise much of the kind of acceptance, love, support and accountability that has been described above. For some, however, Christian discipleship is overshadowed by the sadness that they are not supported at home or among their extended family. They may be the only believer in the household and suffer derision, contempt or downright hostility because they go to church or attend church-related events. Still others have no one close. The housebound can feel totally isolated in their faith. Those in care homes may feel equally isolated unless they find rapport in a carer, visitor or fellow resident.

---

135. Matthew 21:17.

Eva's story

Eva's story may illustrate this circumstance. Eva came from South Africa as a newly married woman to live in England, leaving all her support networks behind. Although she and her husband lived in England they travelled abroad frequently due to his work. Consequently they never really put down roots and had few friends. They had children but they kept their distance over the years.

Following the death of her husband, Eva, in failing health, took up residence in a nursing home. She required continuous oxygen which was supplied through tiny tubes inserted in her nose and which anchored her to her bedroom.

Eva was a woman of serene spirituality and profound faith which was sustained through Bible reading, through prayer book devotions and through watching religious broadcasts on the television. She regarded her television set as her 'lifeline'. Eva was a remarkable witness to the nursing home staff, and bringing her Holy Communion each month was a time of blessing for us both. Was Eva isolated and alone? She never considered herself to be so.

Third Order membership: oblate, alongsider, companion

A more formal and structured way of fostering a healthy spiritual life is by associating oneself with a religious order of a tradition that resonates with one's own spirituality. In previous chapters we have heard how important this is in the life of Brother Andrew who, as a Benedictine oblate, has an identity and a network of support and of learning as well as a structure of prayer, worship and personal devotion.

Sister Helen Julian told us that St Francis began a Third Order for those who could not embrace the full life he modelled. Most religious communities welcome those who are seeking God's will in respect of deepening commitment and offer a meaningful but less binding identification with their order or community. These may be termed 'Companions', 'Associates' or 'Alongsiders'. Most religious communities have a website giving details of how one might visit, stay or work alongside the community.

Spiritual discipline: Rule of life not Rules for life!

It is not only associate members of religious communities who live by a (negotiated) 'Rule of life'. Many Christians find it helpful to design a 'Rule of life': a contract between God and the individual. The word 'rule' comes from a word meaning 'handrail' – something to support us and to help us along the way. A 'Rule of life' will usually comprise a commitment to regular prayer or to a daily 'office': a short liturgy comprising prayers, canticles and readings from the Bible. It may also include a promise to fast at certain times, to receive Holy Communion with particular frequency or to make a retreat, say once each year. If the individual belongs to a Third Order or is attached to a religious community in another way, there may be a commitment to study or to reflect on the writings of the founder. The Rule may also commit the individual to a degree of contact with the community under whose wing their spiritual guidance is governed. Although this may sound daunting to those who enjoy the freedom of designing their own spiritual disciplines, agreeing a Rule of life with a third party can help prevent the Rule being too arduous or unrealistic.

Extreme caution is needed before one makes a commitment to a Rule of life. If we are likely to regularly fall short of the requirements of the Rule, we set ourselves up for a fall and the acquisition of an unnecessary burden of guilt. Once we have promised to God a level of prayerful communication or other disciplines designed to keep us growing in grace and holiness, we begin to regard failure to keep the Rule as a matter of sin. This is one step nearer to the point where the 'sin' of breaking the self-imposed Rule becomes of more concern to us than legitimate sin against God or our neighbour. It becomes more a matter of 'Rule' than a matter of 'Life'! A Rule of life should be for us a climbing frame, not a cage to constrain us.

In his Rule, St Benedict asserts that taking on more than one can deliver is a failing in humility! Being more exacting of ourselves than God expects is a form of pride. We need to view or measure our faithfulness in discipleship through the same lens of love and compassion with which Christ looks upon us. Sometimes the greater challenge or discipline is learning to be kind to ourselves. Returning to the real issues of failure to love God or our neighbour, it could be argued that if we don't know how to be kind to ourselves, we cannot know how to be kind to others.

Designing, promising and keeping a Rule of life is no guarantee of growth in virtue. We can be scrupulous about saying our daily office or fasting twice a week yet be failing miserably in charity, in patience or in kindness. In his book *If You Meet George Herbert on the Road, Kill Him*,[136] Justin Lewis-Anthony asserts that orientation is the essence of a Rule of life: the constant orienting to God and returning to God, time and time again, no matter how many times we fall short. It is reminding ourselves of what we were created for: to love and to serve God, our neighbour and ourselves.

---

136. J. Lewis-Anthony (2009), *If You Meet George Herbert on the Road, Kill Him: Radically Re-thinking Priestly Ministry*, London: Mowbray.

Having offered that 'health warning', and before we rush around the pious practices supermarket with our trolley, dropping in devotional 'goodies', it may be worth reflecting on a few more aids to spiritual health.

Daily prayer

Explicit times of prayer can help frame the day but, as we considered in Chapter two, they are only explications of a deep relationship with God that continues 24 hours a day. In making a commitment to specific prayer times or 'quiet times', we need to be honest with ourselves about how our body clock works and how our household works, being sensitive to the needs of others and with regard to our responsibilities and obligations.

It is worth experimenting with different times of the day for prayer and with the length of time we commit to explicit prayer. An early morning prayer time does not suit everyone. Whatever the time of day the prayer begins it can be considered as opening a conversation with God that continues in many verbal and non-verbal forms until the next explicit prayer rendezvous with God.

Daily office

Participation in the praying of a daily office such as Morning Prayer or Evening Prayer is a way of identifying with the Church universal as it offers prayers to God throughout the day somewhere in the world. A daily office is also a good way to 'frame' our day. It offers a reference point, a time to stop and to bring all we are and all we do, as well as the needs of the world, before God. It can be hard going when said in private. (That is not to say it cannot be irksome and irritating when said or sung in common!)

Bible reading

As we considered in Chapter two, the Holy Scriptures are a major source of life for all Christians. A daily office affords an opportunity to reflect on Scripture. Some may find it beneficial to work to a scheme of Bible reading, perhaps accompanied by notes. These are available through Christian books or through organisations which promote Bible reading, such as the Bible Reading Fellowship.

Spiritual reading

There is a vast range of written material which may serve to nourish us in our spirit, inspire us and encourage us to keep going. Some written material has come down to us from the early centuries of the Church; others, such as the awesome writings of Dietrich Bonhoeffer, come from more recent times. Stories of heroes and heroines of the Church and stories of failure, of rescue, of conversion and of sacrifice can be hugely inspirational. A diet of a little bit of spiritual reading on a regular basis is better than too much too often!

Spiritual direction

There is general agreement amongst writers in the field that spiritual direction is not easy to define and that its meaning is somewhat obscured by the very phrase because what occurs does not necessarily involve 'directing' in any modern sense of the word, nor is the conversation necessarily of a spiritual nature! It has been described as 'one of the more grandiloquent terms that church ministry has inherited from the past'[137] and conjures up an unhelpful image of an ascetic

---

137. W. A. Barry & W. J. Connolly, *The Practice of Spiritual Direction*, New York: HarperCollins, p.9.

monk sitting in a sparsely furnished cell giving a noble lady wise counsel and harsh penances. The term 'soul friend' has been helpful to some,[138] but there are conflicting views on 'friendship' as a dimension of the spiritual direction relationship. Leech insists that the spiritual direction relationship is not an ordinary friendship.[139] It is special both because it stands apart from friends one meets socially and because there is an inequality about it: the director and directee do not, as in a normal friendship, take turns to tell of thoughts, feelings and occurrences. The director listens to the directee and only reciprocates what is shared or disclosed if it is likely to help the directee in some way, and then only sparingly.

There would seem to be almost universal dislike of the term 'directee' for the recipient of spiritual direction. A trawl through spiritual direction-related websites revealed a fashion for the term 'pilgrim'. In the final analysis, however, most authors on the subject settle, reluctantly, for the terms 'director' and 'directee'. For the sake of consistency, therefore, I will do the same.

The first and essential relationship in spiritual direction is that of God and the directee. This relationship is deeper than conscious prayer, though the nature of the prayer relationship with God is of central interest to the director. Gordon Jeff, an esteemed and experienced spiritual director who also trains others in this ministry, asserts 'that it cannot be said too often that the only true director is the Holy Spirit.' He goes on to say that direction, as he understands it, 'is two people sitting down together in an attitude of prayer to try to discern where the Holy Spirit is directing.'[140] Thus a second

---

138. For example, K. Leech (1977), *Soul Friend*, London: Sheldon Press.
139. Ibid.
140. G. Jeff (2007), *Spiritual Direction for Every Christian*, p.12.

human being is introduced into the relationship only, and always, at the invitation of the directee.

Peter Ball states that, at its heart, spiritual direction is about storytelling and listening to stories.[141] The story the director hears may be that of a journey in faith that has been marked by signposts and vistas, by cul-de-sacs and wrong turns. The story may be a current narrative running through the heart and mind of the directee, a dialogue with God that is shared in confidence and trust. There is usually no discontinuity between the narrative the directee has with God and the narrative they are having with the world around them. Some directees will 'test' the relationship with the director with narratives about day-to-day events or relationships at home or at work before entrusting the director with disclosures about a narrative with God. All life is the stuff of spiritual direction.

Margaret Guenther uses powerfully the imagery of 'midwifery' to describe the role of the director in helping to 'birth' the God/directee relationship and the fullness of humanity that it produces.[142] It is arguably Guenther's most abiding contribution to the subject of spiritual direction, embodying as it does a multiplicity of 'helping' roles that include 'teacher', 'encourager', 'confronter', and one who 'rejoices in the "baby"'. Guenther suggests that the way in which midwives work in a place of trust – 'intimate yet professional' – and the way they do things *with* and not *to* people has much to teach us about the role of the spiritual director.

Perhaps we are moving towards Barry and Connolly's definition of Christian spiritual direction, then, as

---

141. P. Ball (2007), *Anglican Spiritual Direction*, New York: Morehouse Publishing.
142. M. Guenther (1992), *Holy Listening: The Art of Spiritual Direction*, London: DLT.

help given by one Christian to another which enables that person to pay attention to God's personal communication to him or her, to respond to this personally communicating God, to grow in intimacy with this God, and to live out the consequences of the relationship.[143]

Adding a little more detail to that definition, Jeff warns us not to try too hard to define it and likens it to a delicate watercolour painting where tints run wondrously into each other.[144]

The director steps carefully and sensitively into the God/directee relationship, bringing with them their own relationship with God and an expectation that the Holy Spirit will be present to both director and directee for the duration of their time together. The director's key disposition is that of 'listener', both to the Holy Spirit and to the directee. Guenther calls this 'holy listening'.[145] Ball quotes Leech who emphasises the 'supreme importance of listening both in direction and in different forms of psychological counselling and therapy',[146] reminding the reader that there is more to listening than hearing and understanding the words with intellect alone. Leech goes on to argue that 'spiritual directors and gurus have always been listeners, but the language to which they listen is the "foreign language" of myths and dreams and symbols, the language of fundamental human experience.'

Guenther suggests that

coming without an agenda, the holy listener is open to anything the directee might bring. She is willing to hear about darkness and desolation, the times of God's seeming

---

143. W. A. Barry & W. J. Connolly, *The Practice of Spiritual Direction*, p.8.
144. G. Jeff, *Spiritual Direction for Every Christian*.
145. M. Guenther, *Holy Listening* (title).
146. K. Leech quoted in P. Ball, *Anglican Spiritual Direction*, p.121.

absence and neglect. She is not frightened by another's anger, doubt or fear; and is comfortable with tears. At the same time the holy listener knows the truth of the resurrection.[147]

Continuing to hear 'the truth of the resurrection' is a discipline for the director who listens to the Holy Spirit for that blessed assurance whilst simultaneously listening to the directee in the throes of the passion. Jeff adds that, at the same time, the director is listening for 'where the Holy Spirit is directing' them both.[148]

But what is the director listening to? In practice, anything! (Remember John in Chapter one?) When a directee arrives for an appointment they may have a well-prepared list of issues and concerns they wish to raise with the director but, in the course of the session (typically one hour long), they may abandon the list and share something that, as a topic, comes as a surprise to both of them. So often this turns out to be 'right' and a result of both of them listening to the Holy Spirit. On the other hand, a directee may arrive for an appointment and declare that they have nothing to talk about and that they had considered cancelling the appointment, only to find that, one hour later, a fruitful conversation has taken place.

Limits on the range of subjects for discussion are set by the limitations in the skill of the director, by their willingness to hear and by the degree to which the directee feels they can trust the director. Although there are no limits to the range of topics of conversation within the spiritual direction relationship, Jeff and others agree with the general advice that the director should be constantly alert to sessions where the presence and activity of God seem to have little to do

147. M. Guenther, *Holy Listening*, p.150.
148. G. Jeff, *Spiritual Direction for Every Christian.*

with the discussion. The general advice is that the director may need to 'probe' for evidence of 'resistance to God.'[149]

It is not the purpose of spiritual direction to address crises. In this, spiritual direction is different from counselling. Jeff makes reference to Leech who assumes that counselling entirely ignores the spiritual dimension, which, Jeff argues, is not always the case.[150] He goes on to identify other differences between the two disciplines. Counselling, he writes, is usually in response to a problem, is generally short term, psychologically oriented and intensive. In contrast, he identifies spiritual direction as being growth centred rather than problem centred and probably continuing for years rather than short term. He understands it to be theologically oriented rather than psychologically oriented and that sessions will be arranged at more widely spaced intervals than would be typical of a counselling programme.

Leech argues that 'spiritual direction is not there for a particular crisis but is even more important when there are no particular crises. It is a continuous ministry and involves the healthy as well as the sick.'[151] Later in the same book Leech admits a relationship between spiritual direction and psychotherapy. He says:

> spiritual direction necessarily involves the psyche: it enters the areas of psychological disturbance and psychological health; it concerns itself with the issues of distress, inner conflict, and upheaval, and mental pain.[152]

Further in the same work Leech makes reference to the spiritual director as helping to 'cast out demons'[153] and as

149. Ibid, p.24.
150. K. Leech, quoted in G. Jeff, *Spiritual Direction for Every Christian*.
151. K. Leech, *Soul Friend*, p.99.
152. Ibid, p.105f.
153. Ibid, p.127.

contrast / compare
psychotherapy v spiritual direction

'healer'.[154] Again, the extent to which these are explored will depend upon the skill of the director and the willingness of the directee.

At one level, there is an ordinariness about direction when one person offers to another a suggestion of how prayer can be approached or how a relationship with God can be developed (the essence of direction in any case). For example, in *Hard Time Praying?* I described the following incident:

> I remember as a young novice monk that I was fidgety and restless during the early morning half hour period of meditation. It was unusual for me to be fidgety because I was usually asleep! On this occasion, however, I was wide awake and aware of every spider on the ceiling of the chapel and every flicker of the pious books of the other monks; every cough and sneeze. I sighed audibly: I even 'tutted' a couple of times. Eventually, the monk kneeling in front of me turned round, looked me straight in the eye. I said, 'I cannot pray.'
>
> He replied, 'Just love him!'

I believe this was a moment of spiritual direction and seemed to require only listening to need, sensitivity, discernment and the confidence to offer a suggestion. The gifts and competences described in the critical literature on the subject, although expansive, may prove to be no more comprehensive than those displayed by my fellow monk. A survey of the gifts and competences cited are worth further consideration. A digest is offered here and with no pretence of ranking in order of importance:

Guenther asserts the supreme importance in direction of listening skills which she recognises as being most well developed in women due to their historic marginality and powerlessness which has engendered an empathy with other

---

154. Ibid, p.134.

'outsiders' which drives their desire to hear.[155] The supreme importance of listening skills is echoed by Ball who quotes Leech on the same subject,[156] and by Jeff.[157] Among other criteria receiving broad approval among key figures are the ability to laugh and to cry with the directee (empathy), the ability to self-disclose when it is appropriate and helpful, and hospitality – offering a 'sacred space' for the God/directee encounter. Guenther intends this space to be both physical and metaphorical. The gift of discernment is valued by Guenther and is discussed under sub-headings of 'perception' and 'judgement'.[158] Other writers concur with this view. Not framed in the same way by other writers consulted for this work is the gift and discipline of waiting, which she states 'can be the most intense and poignant of all human experiences – the experience which, above all others strips us of affectation and self-deception and reveals to us our needs, our values and ourselves.'[159] The tenor of her assertion resonates well with the inspirational writing on the same subject of William Vanstone[160] and Henri J. M. Nouwen's *The Path of Waiting*.

Making confession

The late, great, Michael Ramsey is credited with the comment that, in the Church of England, there are two ways to make one's confession: either to a priest or to our bedspread! Behind this comment are centuries of tradition that recognise both our confidence in the mercy of God

---

155. M. Guenther, *Holy Listening*, p.115.
156. K. Leech, quoted in P. Ball, *Anglican Spiritual Direction*, p.121.
157. G. Jeff, *Spiritual Direction for Every Christian*, p.4.
158. M. Guenther, *Holy Listening*, p.42.
159. Ibid, p.97.
160. W. H. Vanstone, *The Stature of Waiting*.

towards those who turn to God in true repentance and the need for some of us, from time to time, to hear a human voice speaking the words of absolution with the authority of God to do so. This practice is sometimes called the 'Sacrament of reconciliation', since the central motivation is our reconciliation with God following the committal of sin which has drawn us away from that deep communion with God for which we long and hope to enjoy again. There isn't room in this short reflection to go into whether or not making confession of sins to God in the presence of a priest is a sacrament or not. Much depends on what we think a sacrament is! Here I want to commend the practice of making a confession of sins in three circumstances:

1. Sometimes a sin long since committed (and forgiven!) continues to lie heavily upon our conscience. It may be undermining our confidence or inhibiting us from living well the life we have been given. It may be stopping us from serving God in ways to which we now feel called. Under the section 'The Visitation of the Sick' in the *Book of Common Prayer* we find provision for confession to a priest where one's conscience cannot be otherwise quietened.

2. The regular practice of making confession to a priest can be a helpful way of reviewing our Christian discipleship and can be conducted in a relatively informal way, sometimes as part of spiritual direction, prayer for healing or anointing with oil.

3. More frequent confession over a limited period of time can help to tackle a particular habit of sin that is getting in the way of spiritual growth.

A 'first-time' confession needs time for preparation and plenty of time to allow for nervousness or for the difficulty of articulating matters that have lain in the depths, perhaps for several decades. Advice may be needed on how to reflect helpfully and constructively on all that has happened. Breaking the period under review into spans of years can help, as can using the nine-fold fruit of the Spirit[161] or the Ten Commandments as sub-headings for reflection. A sensitive, wise and humble priest will guide a 'penitent' through confession so that it is a life-enhancing and liberating experience.

Making a retreat

Jesus took time apart to commune with his Father, to think through his mission or to recuperate from a time of intense engagement with others. By making a retreat we follow his example. A retreat is time out of one's daily routine. For some it is longed-for quality time with God, a time to think things through or to make a major decision. For others it is a time to catch up on reading or sleep! Retreats fall broadly into four kinds.

First there is the more traditional 'preached' retreat. Over a period of days a retreat leader will offer addresses and lead worship, perhaps on a particular theme. Themed retreats may offer opportunities to explore painting, pottery, embroidery or other arts and crafts. Being creative in the company of others can be very refreshing and inspirational. Led or preached retreats usually include some time in silence, often negotiated between the retreat leader and the retreatants. A good retreat leader will always assert that what

---

161. Galatians 5:22-3.

they have to offer in the way of reflections or addresses should be regarded as optional and should not be allowed to get in the way of what God wants to do with the retreatant in this precious time apart.

A second kind of retreat may be made in the general company of other retreatants, but the retreatant spends most of their time alone with God. Distractions are kept to a minimum and silence is maintained except for meeting with a guide for half an hour or so each day. This is called an 'Individually Guided Retreat' (IGR) and is popular within the Ignatian tradition. An IGR might last a few days, a week or so or, if the full Ignatian Spiritual Exercises are undertaken, for 30 days (see Chapter four). Those offering a 30-day retreat are highly trained and have considerable experience in accompaniment. They will consider applicants very carefully as the full spiritual exercises are very demanding. Those interested in undertaking an IGR are encouraged to begin with a short retreat, then an eight-day retreat, so that they are better prepared to cope with the full 30-day retreat.

A third kind of retreat is where one takes oneself off to a suitable venue, entirely alone, for a few days or even a week. One either caters for oneself or enjoys the hospitality of the venue. This time apart, rather like Jesus going into the desert or up the mountainside, can be very rewarding, though people experiencing retreat for the first time might find it difficult to be completely alone in their own company (and God's company too!) with no one to talk to. In practice, however, if one chooses a retreat centre, a monastery or convent, there is usually someone with whom one can have a conversation if the silence or isolation becomes too much. Alternatively, a short escape from the confines of the location to the nearest pub or café can work just as well!

A fourth kind of retreat has become popular in recent years. It is the so-called 'Retreat in daily life'. Recognising how difficult it can be for some to get away for a retreat, this pragmatic approach to structured reflection in the presence of God may be the answer. In a similar way to the IGR, the retreatant meets regularly with a guide over a period of days or weeks and pledges to spend some time to reflect, usually on scriptural texts suggested by the guide. In the meantime the retreatant goes about their daily life, and the guide pledges to hold them in prayer for the duration of the retreat.

There is much published material on retreat making, and everyone's experience will be different. To bring the reader a sense of balance, I would like to offer a brief account from my own personal experience.

At a particularly busy time in my life I had neglected to organise my annual retreat. The reader will note that I frequently neglect to take my own advice! At that time I was the director of a retreat centre so I was not attracted to making a retreat in a similar establishment: I knew I would spend too much time making comparisons. Having spent some time in religious life I was not in the mood for a convent or monastery. Having secured the necessary time off in my diary I simply set off, vaguely heading for the south coast. I told my wife I would phone when I had found somewhere to stay. So it was that on a cold, blustery day in January I found myself in a resort on the south coast. To my amazement the Tourist Information office was open. I asked the very helpful assistant if she could recommend a place I could stay where I would not be disturbed as I had some work to do. She pointed east and recommended a hotel which was offering a very good low-season deal. Unsure whether I was doing the right thing, I headed for the hotel. I explained what I needed to the person at the reception desk and I was booked into a lovely en-suite room at the top of the building. It even had a view of the sea! Near to the room was a lift that took me straight down to the indoor swimming pool and sauna facilities! When I arrived in the dining room for dinner I was greeted warmly and shown to a table in the corner, laid for one. The food was delicious! I was able to read or to 'people watch' without any time pressure. Short walks were possible, weather permitting, and I was able to pray, reflect, write, soak and sleep to my heart's content. It was quite the best retreat I have ever had, and there was not a religious artefact in sight!

Pilgrimage

We reflected in Chapter two on pilgrimage and the value of the labyrinth as modelling 'journey'. I have included a further note on the subject here to remind us of the value of pilgrimage in providing spiritual nourishment and sustaining spiritual health, and I offer Jeremy's story of his pilgrimage to Santiago de Compostela by way of illustration.

Jeremy's story

The 'journey' (whether in an explicitly spiritual sense or a more subtle self-discovery) is something that all people share in. I get energy from knowing that we are all connected by three common features of life: birth, death and the making sense of everything else in between. This 'making sense of the in-between' is the glue that holds humanity together; it is the common journey of life. From the Christian point of view the *attempting* to make sense of the in-between is the playground for discovering a loving God who delights in journeying with his people.

As we get under way on our pilgrimage we look to encounter God with new eyes and new ways, in people we meet, places we stop, in nature's beauty and our own thoughts and feelings. God is never absent – our delight is in recognising him. To aid us in recognising the One who is always with us we need to put aside our normal way of travelling, which consists of getting from one place to another as quickly and comfortably as possible, and instead, discover the pleasure of moving more slowly and looking more deeply. I began to recognise that there are places that I frequently occupy that also act as places of rest for others, places that others stop at. I also recognise that whilst in these places of rest, others might discover the presence of God. To see this in the micro view of a single encounter is precious, but to realise that this single moment is a stop on a much longer journey with God is humbling; to be treasured and honoured.

As I journeyed between Ponferrada and Santiago I met many different people from many different parts of the world; the age of the pilgrim was just as broad, fourteen to eighty-something I would guess. I found myself walking with people I had never met before and also had the privilege of hearing their stories, of why they chose to take the journey. Some walked the path for spiritual reasons, others for self-discovery, and many for reconciliation or seeking a resolution of sorts.

A common feature of the pilgrimage was a strange start–stop relationship. Meetings and encounters were transitory, often fleeting and brief. If we had time enough to sit and chat it would be over food or a drink and not during the walk. Whilst walking, each pilgrim has their own pace, their own schedule with chosen stop points – unless of course something goes wrong like an injury or similar. This meant that you might meet someone one day but then not see them again for four or five. On meeting again, there is an unusual and surprising joy as if the unsuspecting rendezvous was engineered by God himself. The pilgrimage tricks you into thinking you are meeting a long-lost friend when really you only met the person four days ago. Whether it is a trick or not isn't important; it just goes to highlight the intimacy and the reality of the pilgrimage as the microcosm of life.

Spiritual health: a footnote

Words or phrases such as 'balance' or 'common sense' may be too commonplace to convey their importance in regard to spiritual health. The ability to be kind to ourselves, not to take ourselves too seriously and to maintain a sense of humour and a sense of the ridiculous will carry us much further than will some pious practices. Making time to relax, to rest, to have fun, and making time for intimacy will keep us from scrupulosity and unhealthy introspection. God will keep us spiritually healthy if we will allow it! _Amey_

Whatever we keep by way of disciplines, prayer or worship practices in order to sustain our relationship with God and the world around us, we need to keep it real. Remember that the work of prayer is the sustaining of a relationship with God into which we draw the needs of the world. In sustaining relationships it is not the quantity of attending on another but the quality of that attendance that can be life and relationship enhancing.

Remember that the work of prayer, of support and sustenance for our spiritual welfare, has to be factored into our daily life, our month, our year. Blocking time in our diary for such things is vital and powerful, and we should not feel the need to explain or to justify such things. They are not optional extras!

We have reflected on how we and others identify, experience and express spirituality. We may, too, have reflected on how we have encouraged others on their own journey of discovery. Some of what others have experienced will have resonated with us and some won't. From our smorgasbord of spirituality traditions we have sampled the familiar and the not so familiar. Just because a spirituality tradition is not to our 'taste', it does not mean it is of no value or that it is evil or wrong. Learning to behold what God is doing in others and without judging is an important principle for Christian discipleship and ministry. Remember the Christological commandment to love one another.[162] All else is a working out of that commandment. Love is the only real and everlasting essential Rule of life.

Each tradition has left a legacy to the contemporary Church. Hopefully, by listening and observing how others relate to God and the world around us, we may be able to identify the provenance of expressions of spirituality we encounter. To use a metaphor we encountered in Chapter one, we reflected on how our own spirituality is the fragrance of the essence of us: a spirituality fragrance that is unique to each of us. It is likely to contain the essence of spiritualities that have been valued by the Church for many centuries, a whiff of which we have reflected upon in this book. I hope you may recognise the spiritual fragrance of others even as they may recognise the spirituality fragrance which pervades you. I hope you will find each other, identify with one another and rejoice together in God's goodness.

---

162. John 15:12.

Bibliography

Athanasius, *Against the Arians.*

Ball, P. (2003), *Introducing Spiritual Direction*, London: SPCK.

Ball, P. (2007), *Anglican Spiritual Direction*, New York: Morehouse Publishing.

Barry, W. A. & Connolly, W. J., *The Practice of Spiritual Direction*, New York: HarperCollins.

Blaiklock, E. M. (tr.) (1983), *The Confessions of St Augustine*, London: Hodder & Stoughton.

Brother Ramon and Barrington-Ward, S. (2001), *Praying the Jesus Prayer Together*, Oxford: BRF.

Chapman, J. (1938), *Spiritual Letters*, London: Sheed and Ward.

Clare, J. (2007), *John Clare: Selected by Paul Farley*, London: Faber and Faber Limited.

Cotter, J. (1990), *Healing – More or Less*, Sheffield: Cairns Publications.

Croft, S. (1999), *Ministry in Three Dimensions: Ordination and Leadership in the Local Church*, London: DLT.

De Waal, E. (1999), *Seeking God: the Way of St Benedict*, Norwich: The Canterbury Press.

Durrwell, F. X. (1990), *Mary: Icon of the Spirit and of the Church*, Slough: St Paul Publications.

Meister Eckhart, (1996), *The Wisdom of Meister Ekhart*, New Jersey: Paulist Press.

Foster, R. J. (1998), *Streams of living water: Essential Practices from the Six Great Traditions of Christian Faith*, New York: HarperCollins.

Fry T. (ed.) and Benedict (1981), *The Rule of St Benedict* (*RB80*), Minnesota: The Liturgical Press.

Ganss, G. E. (ed.) (1991), *Ignatius of Loyola: Spiritual Exercises and Selected Works*, New Jersey: Paulist Press.

Goldsmith, M. & Wharton, M. (1993), *Knowing Me, Knowing You*, London: SPCK.

Goldsmith, M. (1994), *Knowing Me, Knowing God*, London: Triangle, SPCK.

Guenther, M. (1992), *Holy Listening: The Art of Spiritual Direction*, London: DLT.

Heywood, D. (2011), *Reimagining Ministry*, London: SCM Press.

Hinton, J. (1992), *Discover your Spirituality*, Rydalmere, NSW: Hunt & Thorpe.

Jeff, G. (2007), *Spiritual Direction for Every Christian*, 2nd edition, London: SPCK.

Julian of Norwich (1976), *Revelations of Divine Love*, Penguin Classics.

Kline, P. (2000), *A Psychometrics Primer*, London: Free Association Books.

Leech, K. (1977), *Soul Friend*, London: Sheldon Press.

Lewis-Anthony, J. (2009), *If You Meet George Herbert on the Road, Kill Him: Radically Re-thinking Priestly Ministry*, London: Mowbray.

Marston, W. M. (1928), *Emotions of Normal People*, London: Kegan Paul, Trench, Trübner & Co Ltd.

Maslow, A. H. (1954), *Motivation and Personality*, New York: Harper.

McGrath, A. E. (1999), *Christian Spirituality: An Introduction*, Oxford: Blackwell.

Michael, C. P. & Norrisey, M. C. (1991), *Prayer and Temperament: Different Prayer Forms for Different Personality Types*, Charlottesville, The Open Door Inc.

Muldoon, T. P. (2004), *The Ignatian Workout*, Chicago: Jesuit Way (Loyola Press).

Nicholl, D. (1981), *Holiness*, London: DLT.

Nouwen, H. J. M. (1995), *The Path of Waiting*, London: DLT.

Perrin, D. B. (2007), *Studying Christian Spirituality*, New York: Routledge.

Rohr, R. (2011), *Falling Upward: A Spirituality for the Two Halves of Life*, San Francisco: Jossey-Bass.

Rohr, R. & Ebert, A. (1990), *The Enneagram: A Christian Perspective*, New York: The Crossroad Publishing Company.

Rolheiser, R. (1998), *Seeking Spirituality: Guidelines for a Christian Spirituality for the Twenty-First Century*, London: Hodder & Stoughton.

Sheldrake, P. (1998), *Spirituality and Theology: Christian Living and the Doctrine of God*, London: DLT.

St John of the Cross, (trans. 1953, reprinted 2003) *Dark Night of the Soul*, New York: Dover publications.

Thompson R. (with Williams, G.) (2008), *Christian Spirituality*, London: SCM.

Tomkinson, R. (2000), *Come to Me: A Resource for Weary Christians and Those Who Care About Them*, Buxhall: Kevin Mayhew Ltd.

Tomkinson, R. (2009), *Hard Time Praying?*, Buxhall: Kevin Mayhew Ltd.

Vanstone, W. H. (1982), *The Stature of Waiting*, London: DLT.

Wakefield, G. S. (ed.) (1983), *A Dictionary of Christian Spirituality*, London: SCM.

Waller, R. & Ward, B. (eds) (1999), *An Introduction to Christian Spirituality*, London: SPCK.

Williams, M. & Penman, D. (2011), *Mindfulness: A Practical Guide to Finding Peace in a Frantic World*, London: Piatkus.

Williams, R. (2002), *Ponder These Things*, The Canterbury Press.

Williams, R. in: R. Waller & B. Ward (eds) (1999), *An Introduction to Christian Spirituality*, London: SPCK.

The Book of Common Prayer, Cambridge University Press.